HERITAGE CRAFTS TODAY

Tole Painting

Tole Painting

Tips, Tools, and Techniques for Learning the Craft

PAT OXENFORD

Photography by Randy Westley

STACKPOLE
BOOKS

To my parents, the late Paul R. Krause and Alethea I. Kennedy Krause
My husband, Ray, and our children, Kelly and Michael

Published by
STACKPOLE BOOKS
5067 Ritter Road
Mechanicsburg, PA 17055
www.stackpolebooks.com

Printed in China

10 9 8 7 6 5 4 3 2 1

FIRST EDITION

Cover design by Tracy Patterson

Frontispiece: Pat Oxenford created this design in acrylic from a tray in the Dr. Richard Godshall collection. The red one-sheet waiter with a white band has yellow peaches with vermilion finger-painted details, blue stroke flowers with leaves along the sides, and yellow sunflowers with vermilion centers and blue strokes on the ends. Vermilion berries and green leaves complete the design. There is no black detail work; the details are painted in deeper shades than the base colors. A yellow stripe is around the inside of the white band, and a double yellow stripe is around the flange.

Library of Congress Cataloging-in-Publication Data

Oxenford, Pat.
    Tole painting : tips, tools, and techniques for learning the craft / Pat Oxenford ; photography by Randy Westley. — 1st ed.
        p. cm. — (Heritage crafts today)
    Includes bibliographical references.
    ISBN 978-0-8117-0431-1 (hardcover, spiral-bound)
    1. Tole painting. I. Title.

TT385.O94 2008
745.7'23—dc22
                                        2008016553

CONTENTS

ACKNOWLEDGMENTS

This book would not have been possible without the support and assistance of many people. A special thank-you to fellow artisan and internationally known Fraktur artist Ruthanne Hartung, for recommending me to share my knowledge of the art of tole painting for this volume of the Heritage Crafts Today series.

I am especially grateful to editor Kyle Weaver at Stackpole Books for his persistence and patience with me. Once I got over the jitters of tackling what seemed a monumental task, it turned out to be worth every effort in getting the job done, and the experience has been one that I never imagined possible.

Thanks to Linda Brubaker, friend, teacher, mentor, and fellow decorative artist, for her encouragement that led me to become a juried member of the Esther Stevens Brazer Guild, Historical Society of Early American Decoration (HSEAD).

I am grateful to several people who allowed me to document and photograph many pieces for this book: Dr. Richard Godshall, who made his tinware collection available; director Stephen Miller and Donna Horst of Landis Valley Museum, who gave me access to the museum's artifacts; and the late Robert and Mary Merritt, Robert J. Merritt Jr., and current president Marjorie Merritt Darrah of Merritt's Antiques in Douglassville, whose help and generosity in sharing many antique pieces with me over the years is unforgettable.

Randy Westley, longtime friend and an outstanding photographer, worked closely with me on this book, taking more than twenty-five hundred photographs, which were narrowed down to get the perfect shots for this book. Without his generously giving of his time and talents, I could not have completed this project. And special thanks to his granddaughter Sydney for her patience and assistance in our Saturday photo sessions. Randy and his wife, Faith, also provided many of their treasures as subjects for the photographs.

Finally, I am indebted to my family for all their support, guidance, and help throughout the years. My parents, the late Paul R. and Alethea I. Krause, always encouraged me to pursue my artistic interests. When I was a young child, my dad sat with me as we drew, colored, carved figures from bars of soap, and painted. My mother taught me to cook, bake, sew my own clothes, crochet, and quilt. They gave me an artist's easel, oil paints, brushes, and books for a birthday present one year to redirect my talents from cake decorating to doing something that would create lasting works of art. I know they are watching over my shoulder as I paint today. I look for those rainbows of their encouragement.

My husband, Ray, encouraged me to focus on studying antique pieces and to try to copy the strokework designs. I immediately enjoyed my newfound interest and have never wavered from studying these old objects. I want to thank him for allowing and helping me to follow my dreams and for being my partner in painting by making the majority of the items I paint.

Our daughter Kelly and son Michael have been patient and understanding of my involvement with painting, and I am honored and pleased to see that they also have artistic talents that are part of their lives, though in different mediums. Thanks also to our son-in-law Matthew and our daughter-in-law Christine, for being supportive as well, and to our grandchildren, Lauren, Erin, and Ryan, who always enjoy painting in Grandmom's studio and who I hope will pursue their artistic talents and continue to enjoy drawing and painting as much as they do now.

INTRODUCTION

Tole is French for sheet iron and originally referred to the heavy-gauge iron trays and metalware items produced and decorated in France during the eighteenth century, though the word today has broader applications. In this book, the term refers to painting on tin. This technique was traditionally used on kitchen items such as trays, coffeepots, teapots, cups and mugs, and canisters, as well as document boxes, trunks, and match safes.

I have been doing decorative painting for more than three decades, with tole painting on tinware being one of my specialties. My work has been displayed at art shows and museums, including two in Germany. I'm a juried member of the Pennsylvania Guild of Craftsmen, a member of the National Society of Decorative Painters, and a Brazer Guild member of the Historical Society of Early American Decoration. I had the privilege of studying with many well-known decorative

Pat Oxenford in her studio with a display of her hand-painted trays.

This gooseneck coffeepot with black background was painted in acrylic by Pat Oxenford, with white flowers and buds and transparent overstrokes of yellow, blue, and red, plus black linework details. Green leaves with yellow veins and strokework complete the design. An elongated S stroke surrounds the top edge of the vessel, and yellow comma strokes are on the bottom flange and lid.

painters, including Jackie Shaw and Jo Sonja Jansen. In 1998, I was selected as one of the top two hundred craftsmen working in traditional forms by *Early American Life*, and I was one of twelve Pennsylvania Dutch artisans featured in the documentary *Expressions of Common Hands: Folk Art of the Pennsylvania Dutch*.

Most of the tinware items I decorate have been handmade by my craftsman husband, Ray, who is a tinsmith, woodworker, and clock repairer. I adapt many of my designs from tracings of those found on old pieces of tinware, painting them on the newly handcrafted pieces.

In this book, I teach you how to do tole painting on your own tinware pieces. The first several chapters talk about the history of tinware and tole painting in America, what tools and materials you need to get started, and the basic skills used by traditional tole painters. You will learn how to prepare your tin for painting and how to make the basic strokes and folk-art flowers, then move on to specific projects that incorporate what you've learned. There are also galleries of early and reproduction painted tinware that you can copy or use for inspiration to create designs of your own.

A Brief History of Tole Painting

The folk art of painting on tinware, known as tole painting, was first done in New England just after the Revolutionary War. It became popular among the Pennsylvania Dutch when tin peddlers carried unpainted wares from the New England tinsmiths as far as Virginia to sell to a wider market. Before I talk about painting on tinware, let's take a look at the early tinshops, where they were located, what they made, and what characteristics defined each of them.

In the early 1700s, German and Swiss immigrants settled in Pennsylvania, about the same time that Edward Pattison arrived from Wales and settled in Connecticut, near the Berlin-Hartford area, where he established the first known tinshop in the colonies around 1740. This region soon became the center of the American tin industry and remained so until around 1850. Pattison imported his raw materials of tinplate, wire, and lead from Pontypool, Wales. These raw materials were

Above: This half-sheet waiter measures 8³/₄ x 6 inches. It has a black background, with a semitransparent white border around the edge of the floor. The design consists of green leaves with black strokework detail and red berries. A fine yellow stripe is around the inside edge of the white band on the floor, with a series of three graduating-size comma strokes around the inside. A yellow rickrack stroke border complements the flange. PRIVATE COLLECTION

Painted with a red base, this oblong bread tray has a white band around the floor. The ends each have a large yellow ball flower and two large yellow leaves with black details, along with a series of comma strokes to form the smaller leaf details. The side design has a single row of yellow teardrop strokes along the bottom edge and a series of two comma strokes near the top edge. The design on the white band on the floor is green leaves with red berries and fine black linework details.
PRIVATE COLLECTION

A vermilion ball flower, with yellow and semitransparent white comma-overstroke details, is the main feature of this large black oval spice canister. At the base of the flower are two large green comma strokes. Three stylized green leaves with yellow detail plus clusters of yellow comma strokes and dots complete the design. Note the fine yellow cross-hatching at the center top of the ball flower between the comma strokes. A yellow rickrack border enhances the top of the canister, and a spray design of yellow comma strokes appears on the top of the lid. PRIVATE COLLECTION

first brought into the colonies through Boston Harbor, but as the tinsmithing trade became popular, merchants in New York also began to stock the raw materials.

At first Pattison worked alone to make enough products to both sell from his shop and peddle around the local countryside. These silvery household items were greatly admired, and business grew as more and more people bought them to replace those made of horn, wood, iron, and pewter. When young men of the area realized that the tinsmithing business was a good trade, they were eager to become apprentices. The tin industry grew so fast and was so successful that each tinsmith soon acquired his own apprentices, and it wasn't long until most homes in the Berlin area had a trained tinsmith. Over the next century, the industry came to involve a large part of the population of Hartford County.

These early tinshops were small and often located in the dooryards of the tinsmiths' homes, allowing them to continue to do their farm chores, since the families lived off the land. Pattison taught his apprentices to make what he did, and they in turn handed down these forms to their successors. Many of the tin objects were fashioned after practical English pottery and metalware, though occasionally new items were introduced by a tinsmith. Pattison's shop was known for trays, coffeepots, teapots, document boxes and trunks, canisters, and small cradles.

This red sugar bowl has a white band around the top with green leaves that have black detail and red berries. A yellow rickrack design with double yellow dots is directly below the white band. There are yellow teardrop strokes around the bottom flange and yellow stroke details on the dome top.
PRIVATE COLLECTION

Featuring an asphaltum background, this syrup cup has a large vermilion ball flower in center front and a smaller vermilion ball flower on each side, with alizarin crimson and yellow comma-stroke detail. Leaves are yellow and green comma strokes, and a fine yellow stripe encircles the bottom edge. The lid has yellow comma-stroke details.
PRIVATE COLLECTION

There were several other important early tinshops. Elijah and Elisha North operated tinshops from 1806 to 1840 in Maine. Another prominent tinsmith in Maine was Oliver Buckley, whose shop was in operation from 1807 through 1855. The Buckley shop is known for the platform-top document box as well as the wet-on-wet technique of painting found on early document boxes, tea caddies, and teapots. By 1830, Zachariah Stevens had established a tinshop in Stevens Plains, Maine, where he had a thriving business until 1842. (Stevens's great great granddaughter, Esther Stevens Brazer, wrote the influential book *Early American Decoration* in 1940, causing a resurgence of interest in decorative painting. The Historical Society of Early American Decoration was founded in her memory in 1946.)

The first of the Filley tinshops was operated by Oliver Filley from 1800 to 1846 in Bloomfield, Connecticut. From 1818 through 1853, Harvey Filley had a tinsmith shop in Philadelphia. In 1825, Augustus Filley opened another shop in Lansingburg, New York. The Filley shops were noted for the variety of items they produced, including several kinds of trays, canisters, coffeepots, sugar bowls, creamers, molasses or syrup cups, knitting needle cases, tumblers, snuffer trays, candleholders, snuffboxes, and match safes.

The early tinplate was not like that which we use today. It was hand dipped, which gave it an uneven or wavy-looking texture. The early tinplate sheets meas-

This alphaltum mug is 4^1/$_4$ inches tall and 3^1/$_4$ inches in diameter, with a semitransparent white band around the top edge. The center front has a scalloped-edge vermilion flower with yellow center, with a four-petal vermilion flower and three vermilion buds on each side. The petal flower has alizarin crimson and yellow details plus green stroke leaves. Yellow comma strokes form the border along the edge of the white band. PRIVATE COLLECTION

The top decoration on this flat-top yellow document box consists of two stylized red roses and three red rosebuds with green leaves and black veins. A fine black stripe surrounds the top edges, while fine double black stripes surround the top edge and lower bottom. The piece measures 6 1/2 inches long, 3 1/2 inches wide, and 2 3/4 inches high. PRIVATE COLLECTION

ured only 10 x 14 inches, so large waiters, or trays, had to be seamed in the middle, thus the term two-sheet waiters. The sheets of tin also were not large enough to make the vessel part of a coffeepot, so a triangular gore of tin had to be inserted and soldered at the bottom backside under the handle. Today sheets of tin are 24 x 36 inches, and long rolls of tin are also available. But to be historically correct, when modern tinsmiths make gooseneck coffeepots or two-sheet waiters, they will cut the tinplate in the same way as the early tinsmiths.

Early pieces made prior to the Revolutionary War were sold plain, without any decorative painting. As the New England tin peddlers sold the pieces to families further south, the ladies of the household would decorate them. Especially in the Berks and Lancaster County area, the Pennsylvania Dutch women became very proficient in decorating tinware, with red being their primary background color. After the war, the English art of japanned and flowered tinware was introduced, and it became the preferred tinware. Most of the early paint decorators did not sign their work, so we cannot identify them. Some early tinware pieces may have a signature or name scratched into the bottom, but it is thought that this is the name of the owner rather than the painter of the piece.

The painting and decorating of tinware at the shops was usually done by women and girls, who enjoyed the art, although a few boys also painted and decorated tinware. The girls were given six-week apprenticeships, during which they had to learn the technique of country painting on tin, the brush strokes to form the motifs, striping, and all other aspects of the decorative-painting trade before they were permitted to lay a brush to a piece of tinware. It was felt that brush control was more important than artistic ability. The designs were of light, quick brush strokes in various combinations to form flowers, leaves, borders, and striping. Once proficient, a painter could earn as much as $1.25 per week.

Just as each tinshop had its own style of design of the tin objects, their decorative painters also had their own styles, though the technique of base-coating the objects before any decoration was applied was the same. The process that was used by the early decorative painters is referred to as japanning. This term reflects the English decorators of the seventeenth century who worked to imitate the Oriental lacquerware imported into Europe at that time. Sometimes people also refer to the early tinware as japanware.

The early pieces were generally painted with black backgrounds until 1815, when red and blue were introduced as background colors. Following the discovery and refining of petroleum, asphaltum—a semitransparent brownish black or reddish brown oil color—was used for backgrounds. The amount of color pigment

and the amount of varnish added to the asphaltum determine how transparent the color is. Asphaltum allows the sheen of the new tin to glow through, and old tinware with asphaltum is highly sought after today.

Paint did not come in tubes as it does today. The pigments were very expensive, and they were mixed with varnish to make both the background colors and the paints for the decorative designs.

Today historians can determine what pieces were painted by each of the well-known tinshops, even though most pieces were not signed. Design of the tinware, choice of colors, and design of the decoration are key factors.

The Pattison tinshops frequently used red or vermilion, a salmon pink, as the basecoat of the ball-type flowers. Their early designs were a simpler, more primitive style than the more complex and detailed designs that appeared later. They used shades of medium, dark, and olive for strokework details and leaves; light, medium, and dark yellow or ochre for strokework, detail on leaves, borders, and striping; alizarin and transparent white for overstrokes on flowers; and opaque white for cross-hatching. They rarely used blue, but if they did it was a medium blue. Black was occasionally used for details on the flowers, leaves, or squiggles. Pattison tinshop designs were usually geometrically balanced and consisted of ball-type flowers or a combi-

This very elegant gooseneck coffeepot measures 10¹/₂ inches tall and 6¹/₂ inches in diameter. It has an asphaltum background and a large white semitransparent circle on both front and back. Three vermilion flowers with yellow and black details and one yellow flower with green, vermilion, and black details along with green leaves complete the circular design. Yellow comma strokes encircle the white circle. At the top is a narrow ¹/₂-inch yellow band with small thin black comma strokes, and groups of five comma strokes surround the bottom flange of the coffeepot. Note the brass knob for the lid handle, characteristic of the gooseneck coffeepot, and the inset gore from beneath the handle to the bottom flange. The details on the lid are clusters of yellowstroke work to complement the bottom flange and a starburst design around the brass knob.
PRIVATE COLLECTION

nation of balls or heart shapes to form a flower. These flowers had overstrokes to create the detail, and some had side petals to complete the flower form. Leaves were pointed or round forms, had yellow veins, and often had yellow squiggles for details. Borders were stroke-work detail, but rarely was striping used on these early pieces.

The Filley shops, especially the one in Philadelphia, used black, asphaltum, and red as their base or background colors. They also introduced the art of crystalliz-

13

ing their base coats. This process was the first step in base or background painting. Alizarin crimson and varnish were randomly brushed on in a slip-slap fashion to the area that was to be crystallized, often the floor of a cut-corner tray. The object was then baked in an oven. It was watched very closely as the oven temperature was gradually increased to 380 degrees, then cooled down. During this heating and cooling process, the color changed from reddish and burgundy to shades of golden yellow or brownish tones. This was no easy feat, as the ovens were usually in the open hearth of a fireplace. Another distinctive feature of Filley shop tinware is the use of painted white bands around the floor of a tray or on a document box or trunk. These white bands have overstrokes of floral designs with fine details, as well as black squiggles. The Filley shops also introduced the color blue into these border designs. On coffeepots, especially the gooseneck coffeepots, they painted white circles or crescents that also included overstrokes of beautiful floral designs.

It was a long process to paint an item back then, as it still is today for those who use oil paints. Usually the decorative painter worked on several pieces at once, in various stages of decoration.

After proper preparation of the tin was completed, the background color was applied. This had to dry thoroughly, taking as long as several days, before the decorative design painting or strokework began.

The base color of the design was painted first, such as vermilion for the ball-type flowers. This had to dry a minimum of twenty-four hours before the first set of overstrokes could be applied, such as alizarin, and possibly some of the green strokes. These strokes could not overlap or touch other strokes that were still wet, and it took a minimum of twenty-four more hours before the next strokes could be applied.

The next step would be the white overstrokes. This white was sometimes just painted next to the previously painted strokes, but white pigment is usually very transparent and allows the underneath color to show through. Any cross-hatching strokes were also painted at this time.

Often yellow strokes were used along with or as overstrokes on the green leaves and stems. Yellow was also a popular color for striping and flange borders. Here again, after each color, the previous paint had to dry for twenty-four hours before applying the next color. If decorative curlicues or squiggles were included in the designs, they were completed before the striping and borders.

Once all the decoration was completed and thoroughly dry, the piece needed to be varnished to seal and preserve the design. Several coats of varnish were applied, with proper drying time and wet-sanding between coats, in order to properly preserve the design. We still do this today, just as in earlier times.

Tools and Materials

The early pieces of tinware were decorated with oil paints and mediums. You may find it easier, however, to work with acrylic paints and mediums. Below I've listed tools and materials for both.

OIL PAINTS
There are many different brands of oil paints, each with a wide range of colors.

OIL-PAINT STRIPING BRUSHES
If you use oil paints, you'll need oil-painting striping brushes. When properly dressed with the paint, these brushes leave a very fine stripe line.

Oil vs. Acrylic

These two half-sheet waiters have the same design; however, the design on the left was completed in oils, while the one on the right was done in acrylics. The two white central flowers are overpainted with yellow, vermilion, and black details. The green leaves and red berries have yellow details. A yellow stripe is around the edge of the floor, and comma strokes, dots, and a yellow stripe are around the flange. COLLECTION OF RAY AND PAT OXEN-FORD

QUILLS

Quills are the type of brushes that were employed by the early decorators of tinware and are used primarily with oil paints. Both round and flat quills are available in many sizes. I prefer to store my quills in an enclosed box so that they are flat when not in use. You can purchase special brush boxes at art-supply stores for this purpose.

ACRYLIC PAINTS

Today artist acrylic paints and mediums are also available from many different companies, and here too there are many colors in both tubes and bottles to choose from. I paint in both mediums. I have tried many different brands of acrylic paints and mediums over the years, but I prefer the JoSonja's products.

MEDIUMS

There are several mediums you can mix with the paints:
- Flow medium for thinning the paint to the consistency you need.
- Kleister medium to give the paint a transparent look for overstroke work.
- Satin varnish to complete the project with a protective coat.
- Gel retarder to antique an item.

These are just a few of the mediums available in JoSonja's line of products.

STAY-WET PAINT BOX

Storing the paint in use for a particular project in a stay-wet paint box keeps it fresh for weeks. Keep the sponge moist and the lid on the box when not in use.

WAXED PALETTE

A waxed palette is a great surface on which to mix paints and dress the brush with paint.

17

BRUSSHES

You need various sizes of many kinds of brushes, such as flats, rounds, filberts, liners, and stripers for different types of strokes. Whether you decide to paint with oils or acrylics, purchase good-quality brushes; your finished product is only as good as the quality of your brushes.

WATER CONTAINER

A container for water, especially when using acrylic paints, is needed to clean your brushes, and this one on the right in the picture above has had many years of use. A good way to clean the dried-on paint from your water basin is to put a few drops of dishwasher soap in the bottom of the water basin, fill to the top with water, and heat in your microwave oven for a few minutes. Dispose of the dirty paint water, and your basin will be clean again. (Do not pour it down a drain, as you can clog up the system.) The basin has ridges in the larger end to rub your brush to remove excess paint. You can also store your brushes in the holes around the top edge of the basin.

WOODEN BRUSH HOLDER

I prefer to store the brushes I am using for a project on a wooden brush holder. Ray made these holders by cutting dowel rods in half and filing grooves in which the brushes can rest.

PICK BOARD HEART

Pick boards often come in the shape of a heart and are used to remove paint from your brushes. Work soap into the bristles and then run them back and forth across the pick board to loosen the paint.

PALETTE KNIVES

Palette knives, which come in many sizes and styles, are used to mix paint colors or blend mediums into your paints.

SPRAY BOTTLE

A spray bottle is handy for misting the paint and keeping the underneath sponge or shop towels moist in the paint box so that the paints stay fresh and usable.

TINWARE

You'll need to obtain some reproduction tinware that is unpainted or raw tin, such as this miniature document box, straight-spout coffeepot, Betty lamp, oil filler pot, candle sconce, and napkin holder. All of these pieces were made by Ray (see page 165).

You also could use hot dipped tin pieces, which are still being manufactured today, though they're somewhat hard to find. Hot dipped tin has a wavy appearance and is elegant just left unpainted. You can see this wavy appearance on the tapered cup, candle sconce, and Betty lamp, which are just polished, with no preservative, decorations, or varnish on them. Ray made these pieces as well.

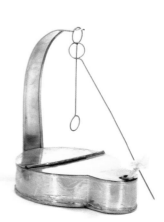

SHOP TOWELS

Blue shop towels are great for blotting your brushes. I like to cut them into smaller pieces to keep beside my palette or paint box. You can also use them in your stay-wet paint box, along with waxed paper, as described below.

WAXED PAPER

To prepare your stay-wet paint box, cut several blue shop towels to fit into the box. Thoroughly wet the towels, squeeze out the excess water, and cover with a sheet of deli-wrap dry waxed paper. Fold the waxed paper around the towels, tuck in the ends, and place into your paint box.

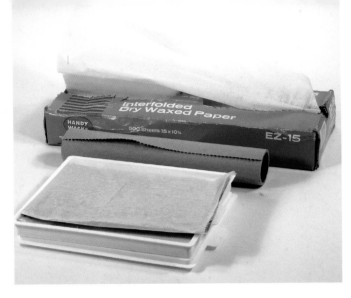

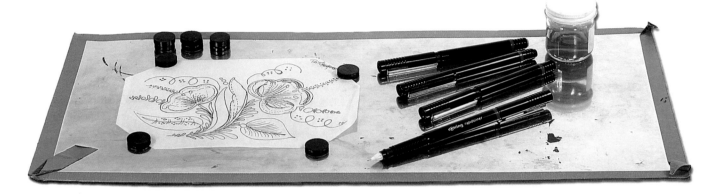

SHEET TIN AND MAGNETS

Pieces of sheet tin in various sizes are great for preparing your tracing paper patterns. Cover the edges with tape before using. Then use small magnets to hold the tracing paper and pattern in place. These magnets can be purchased in craft stores and are usually packaged in tubes of about twenty-four.

TECHNICAL PENS

Technical pens with permanent ink are ideal for making your pattern tracings.

GLASS CLEANER

Keep a small jar of Windex or other liquid glass cleaner on hand, and dip the pen tip into it if it becomes clogged or the ink won't flow.

TRANSFER PAPER

Transfer paper comes in both sheets and rolls. An inexpensive way to make your own is to cut out black portions of advertisements from newspapers. This works well for transferring patterns, especially onto a white or light background.

STYLUS

A stylus is a tool for tracing over the pattern lines to transfer the design onto the object to be painted. It has a fine point on one end and a somewhat heavier point on the opposite end. You could also use an old ballpoint pen that no longer has ink to trace the design, although a stylus is somewhat finer and easier to use.

SANDPAPER

Cut sheets of 600-grit, 1,200-grit, and 1,500-grit sandpaper into small squares, rounding the corners so that you do not jab them into the object while you are sanding.

DISHWASHING LIQUID

In a small plastic container, mix a drop or so of Palmolive or other dish liquid into some water, and keep it on hand for preparing your wet sandpaper.

SCRUFFY PADS

Various stiffnesses of scruffy pads (white, burgundy, and green) are also used for sanding purposes.

TACK CLOTH

A tack cloth is used to remove the paint dust after sanding each coat.

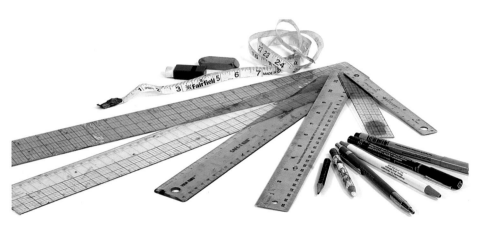

RULERS AND MEASURING TAPE

Flexible plastic rulers and metal rulers with cork backing in various sizes are important tools for making patterns and laying out your design on an object. A cloth measuring tape is helpful when working on a round object such as a coffeepot.

PENCILS AND PENS

Drawing pencils, chalk pencils, and pens are essential for drawing, tracing, and marking.

ERASERS

Kneaded and pink pearl erasers are used for removing drawn lines from an object.

WASTE BAGS AND PAINTER'S TAPE

Fold down the top edge of a small waste bag and attach it to your work area with blue painter's tape. Use it to discard paper towels used for anything that is smelly or of a hazardous nature, such as oil paints, mediums, or turpentine. At the end of your painting session, unfold the top, squeeze out all the air, and tightly tie or knot the top. Dispose of properly in a metal trash can with a tight-fitting lid or a hazardous waste container. For my waste bags, I recycle the plastic sleeves from newspapers.

VARNISH

Varnish is used as a medium with oil paints and also as a finish coat once the decoration is completed. To keep a skin from forming on the top of the varnish in the container, turn the can upside down, punch a small hole in the bottom near the edge, and insert a screw eye. To get varnish from the can, remove the screw eye, turn the can over, and allow the varnish to flow out of the hole.

VARNISH BRUSH

You need a 1- to $1^1/2$-inch flat brush to apply the varnish.

TELEPHONE BOOKS

Old telephone books make a great surface for working the varnish into the brush, as well as cleaning the varnish from the brush when you are finished.

PRIMER

Rustoleum red primer is used for the first coat of paint on all your tinware pieces, before applying the base coat that will serve as the background color.

FOAM BRUSHES

You'll need several 1-inch foam brushes for applying the primer and base coats.

BRIDGES

Bridges in various sizes help keep your hand off the painting surface. Ray made various sizes from wood, but you can purchase commercially made bridges.

METAL CANS, SMALL PAPER CUPS, NYLON STOCKINGS, AND PLASTIC SPOONS

Recycle your metal cans, especially tomato paste and tuna fish cans, for use when painting. Small paper cups fit into the tomato paste can, to strain paint. Cut old nylon stockings into squares, stretch over the top of cup and can, secure with a rubber band, and strain your varnish or paint to remove any specks of dirt or unmixed paint. A plastic spoon is helpful for measuring paint from a can and also depressing the nylon stocking when straining paint. Recycled metal cans can also be used for storing brushes.

LIDS

Miscellaneous lids are good for holding small amounts of specially mixed colors or painting mediums. You also can use the larger lids as covers over individual oil paints that you've mixed with the varnish medium when painting. This helps keep your oil paint fresh longer, so that it does not dry out so quickly. A nutcracker is handy for removing paint tube caps that can be difficult to open.

ACETATE

Dura-Lar is a clear acetate that is great for making a permanent painted pattern or for covering a painted pattern that is preserved on black cardboard. Bristol board and vellum are other types of painting surfaces on which you can prepare patterns or practice designs.

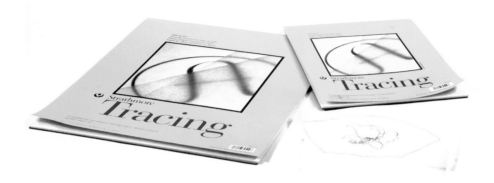

TRACING PAPER

Tracing paper, in a variety of sizes, is the paper of choice for making the line-drawing pattern to trace onto the object to be painted.

LIGHTBOX

A lightbox is an excellent tool that helps you see the design through the tracing paper when creating your patterns. It's an expensive item, but if you are a serious painter, you'll most likely invest in a lightbox. They come in a variety of sizes.

BABY OIL AND BATH OIL

Work some baby oil into your quills after they are properly cleaned to prepare them for storage. If you forgot to clean a brush properly, work some Avon Skin So Soft into the bristles. It helps soften the dried-on paint.

WIPES AND PAINTER'S SWIPES

When working with acrylics, use moist wipes such as Wet Ones to wipe off smudges of paint and clean your hands. Oops! Painter's Swipes are good for cleaning your hands when working with oil paints.

ENAMEL PAINTS

Enamel paints called 1 Shot in black, yellow, and red are used in oil painting. They are mixed with varnish and tinted with tube oils to create the desired color, especially yellow.

LIGHTER FLUID AND COTTON SWABS

Ronsonol lighter fuel is used sparingly on a cotton swab to remove any yellow 1 Shot paint that you placed incorrectly. Use it as soon as you realize you made a mistake. Yellow enamel will leave a yellowish haze on the surface if not properly removed.

TURPENTINE OR MINERAL SPIRITS

Turpentine or mineral spirits is used to clean oil paint from your brushes or quills. Keep the cap secured tightly while not in use. I like to keep a small amount in a clear glass jar prominently marked with the contents and swish my brush in it to clean. Make sure the lid on the jar is secure when not using.

ROLCO VARNISH

Rolco is another type of varnish that can be mixed with oil paints. As with the other varnish, use a screw eye in a hole in the bottom of the inverted can to keep a skin from forming over the medium.

DRYING OVEN

I prefer to dry my tinware in a drying oven to keep it dust-free and to speed the process of drying or curing the paint. Ray and I transformed two nitrogen etching ovens into drying ovens by removing the etching equipment and converting it to electric. We use a 100-watt lightbulb for the heat source. Each oven has multiple pullout drawers and a glass door.

Basic Skills

This chapter will teach you the basic skills you
need to paint your own toleware. Once you have
practiced and mastered these skills, you can put them
together to create the projects later in this book.

When preparing the tinware project for painting, and whenever using oil paints, always work in a well-ventilated area. An electric room air purifier is also helpful for removing the smell of the oil paints and other mediums and solvents.

Begin by using a medium scruffy pad (burgundy color) to rough up the smooth, shiny tin surface. This helps the paint to adhere to the smooth surface.

Wipe down the tin surface with turpentine, alcohol, or mineral spirits to remove any oil or solder flux. Even oil from your hands can leave a greasy film on the tin.

The next step is to prime the tin with Rustoleum red primer. Stir the contents of the can well with a popsicle stick. It's a good idea to strain the primer. I strain it through a piece of old nylon stocking into a small paper cup placed inside a recycled tomato paste can. Then, using a plastic spoon, measure out 2 spoonfuls of paint and 1 spoonful of turpentine, and stir. Check the consistency of the primer, which should be thin. Now brush a thin coat of the primer onto one side only of your tinware, using your sponge brush. Start in the center, working to the edge of the object. If you're painting a tray, do the outside rim last. Allow the primer to dry, and then do the reverse side.

When drying tinware, I like to use a drying oven to make sure that no moisture remains in the seams or edges of the piece. This also helps the paint cure and adhere to the surface. I have two converted drying ovens that are each powered by a 100-watt lightbulb. Each oven has three pull-out shelves and allows things to dry in a dust-free environment. You can use the heat of the lightbulb in the oven of your stove, but be extremely careful that the oven temperature is not turned on.

Before painting an object, it is very important that the surfaces be smooth. Likewise, between steps in the painting process, it is necessary to sand the painted surface. Wet-sanding is my preferred method. Once the primer on both sides is dry, sand with a small piece of 600-grit wet sandpaper. First soak the sandpaper in a small, shallow container of water with a drop or two of dish liquid for about fifteen to twenty minutes before use. It's best to sand lengthwise, and sand in one direction only. Check for smoothness by running your fingertips over the surface. Once it's sanded smooth enough that you can't feel any bumps or ridges, rinse the object under running water, and dry thoroughly.

Now your piece is ready for the base coat. Secure the object you will be base-coating to the pick boards. Thin and strain the paint as directed in the primer step. Then use a sponge brush to apply the base coat color. This usually requires a minimum of two coats of paint.

Wet-sand after each coat, followed by the use of a tack cloth to remove the paint dust. Once the desired base-coat color is achieved and you've sanded it smooth, seal the paint with a barrier or varnish coat. Use varnish over oil paint or JoSonja's Clear Glaze over acrylic. If you make a mistake or decide you do not like the placement of your design, it's much easier to remove if the paint has a barrier coat applied. This also keeps the decorative painting from seeping into the base coat. Follow the manufacturer's directions, and it's also a good idea to strain the varnish just as you did the primer and base-coat paints. Allow the object to dry a minimum of 24 hours before wet-sanding again.

Once you have prepared your tinware surface properly, it is time to proceed with the decorative process.

Tips for Painting

- Long fingernails and tole painting on tinware do not go well together. Long fingernails will click on the tinware and possibly scratch the surface before it is cured. It's a good idea to keep your fingernails no longer than the ends of your fingers.
- Avoid wearing clothing that sheds a lot of lint, or is fuzzy, such as a sweater.
- Lint and dust particles do not get along well with the decorative painter.

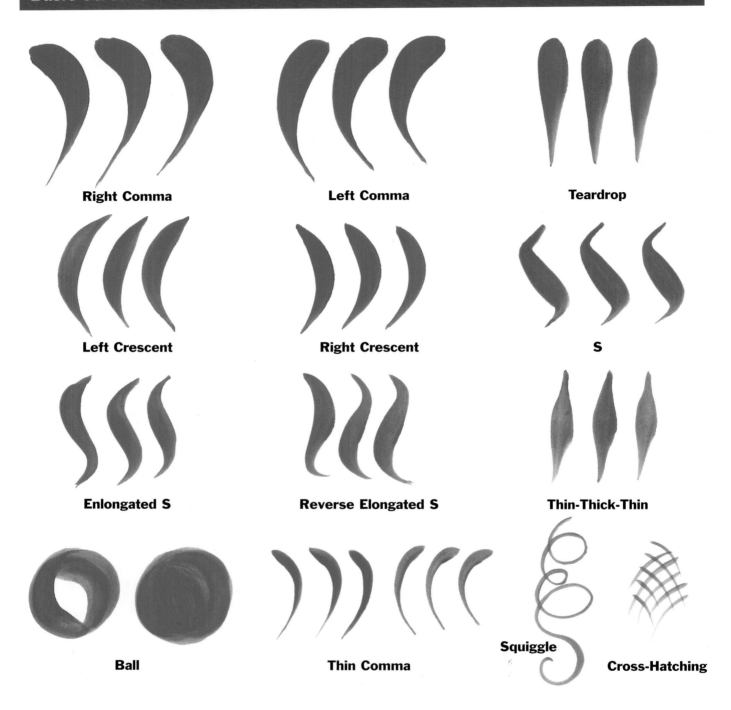

Right Comma   Left Comma   Teardrop

Left Crescent   Right Crescent   S

Enlongated S   Reverse Elongated S   Thin-Thick-Thin

Ball   Thin Comma   Squiggle   Cross-Hatching

If you are a first-time painter, before you begin a project, spend some time studying the photographs of the basic strokes. Then practice the strokes on newspaper, bristol board, or white gift-box cardboard with a somewhat shiny surface, or even tracing paper. You can place a piece of clear acetate topped with a piece of tracing paper over the brush strokes in this book, and paint over them to help you get the feel of the strokes. I cannot stress enough the importance of practice in learning the basic strokes.

Use a number 4 round brush to begin practicing the strokes in this section. The first step is to load your brush with paint. To do this, dip the tip of the round brush into the edge of the paint puddle on the palette, and gently work the brush back and forth to load it. When painting, whenever possible, try to use a bridge for your hand so that it does not get into anything you have previously painted that may still be wet. You can also rest your little finger on the painting surface to help steady your hand.

The comma stroke is a basic one in folk-art painting.

To begin the right comma stroke, place the brush on the surface at the 12 o'clock position.

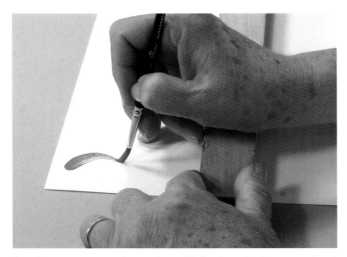

Apply pressure and gently pull the brush down to the 6 o'clock position.

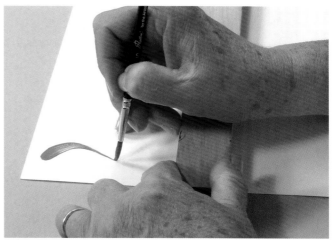

As you pass 3 o'clock, begin to gently release pressure to form the tail of the stroke, lifting up at the 6 o'clock position.

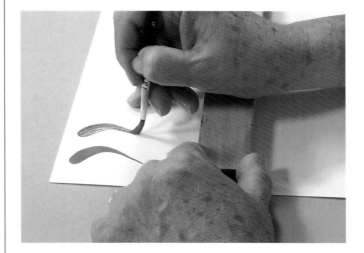

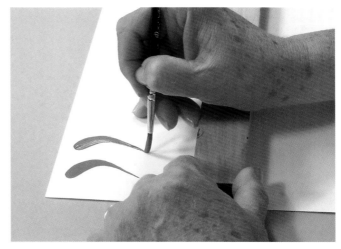

If you are making several of these strokes, you'll need to adjust the work so that you begin at 12 o'clock and end at 6 o'clock.

Pull the stroke across to the 3 o'clock position.

The left comma stroke is done the same way, except that you turn your work and begin at the 9 o'clock position.

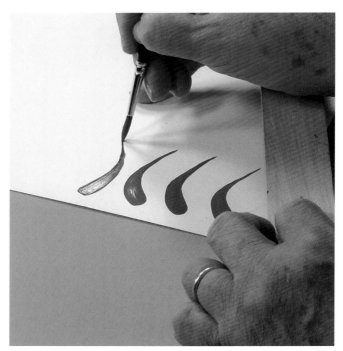

As you pass 6 o'clock, gently release the pressure and pull the brush to a point at 3 o'clock. Note how the worksheet position was changed to facilitate this movement.

Whereas the comma stroke is slightly curved, the teardrop or straight comma stroke is straight.

Here you pull the stroke straight down from 12 to 6 o'clock, but do not flare the stroke out to the side. It's one straight movement—press, pull, release.

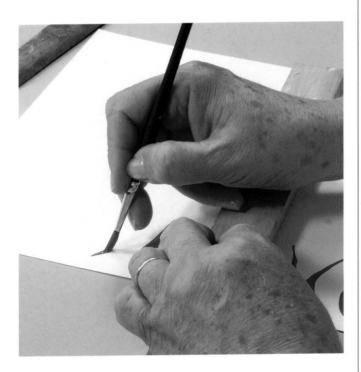

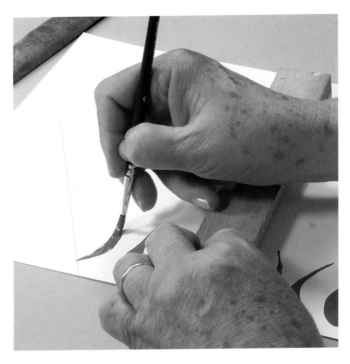

The left crescent stroke is pulled from 9 to 3 o'clock. Touch the surface, pull, apply pressure, pull, and release. This process creates the fullest part of the stroke in the central section.

The right crescent stroke is pulled from 12 to 6 o'clock, turning your work to facilitate this movement. Tip the brush to the surface at 12 o'clock, pull, apply pressure, pull, and release the brush at 6 o'clock. Look at the practice stroke sheet as a reference.

Resting the brush on the tip, or chisel edge if using a flat brush, creates the S stroke. Gradually increase the pressure as you change directions slightly. Begin to release the pressure as you change the direction again, ending on the tip or chisel edge. Do not twist the brush to form this stroke, but change directions instead. This can be done with either a left or right starting point.

The elongated S stroke is basically done the same way as the regular S stroke, except that a little more pressure is applied at the beginning and end, making the stroke a little fuller.

It can be done from either the left or right starting point.

This thin-thick-thin stroke is created by pulling down in a straight line from 12 to 6 o'clock. Start on the tip of the brush, gradually increase pressure as you are pulling midpoint, and then begin to decrease the pressure as you end the stroke.

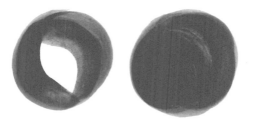

There are several ways to make a filled-in ball. An easy method is to use a series of comma strokes to complete a circle and fill it in.

Turn the object upside down and make another right comma stroke to form the basis for the circle.

Begin with a right comma stroke.

Then fill in the center by doing one or two more comma strokes, depending on the size of your circle.

Once you feel as though you're comfortable with these strokes, move to a number 2 liner brush to make thinner strokes. A liner brush has just a few hairs, which are slightly longer than those on the fuller round brush.

Practice some comma strokes with the liner brush to get the feel of it.

The comma stroke is created the exact same way as when using the number 4 round brush.

Next try some squiggles or curlicues with the fine liner brush. The paint should be thin; add some flow medium to thin your paint slightly if using acrylics. You want the paint to be able to flow easily from the tip of your brush.

The brush is held perpendicular to the object to be painted, and only the tip is touching.

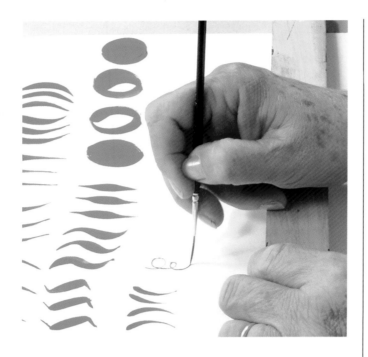

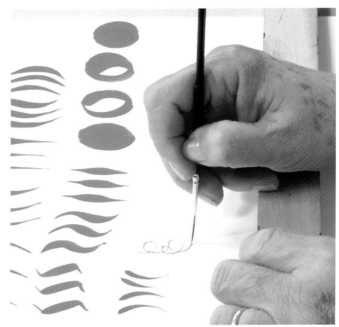

Freely move your brush in circles, varying the sizes of the circles slightly and in some instances even the direction in which you make the circles, and end with a curved line. These should be fun; just relax, and keep your wrist flexible and the movements fluid and steady.

Cross-hatching is also done with the liner brush. It looks best when done on a diagonal and with an uneven number of lines, such as three or five. The lines can be straight or slightly curved. Whichever way you start, all lines should be the same.

Start the lines at the top of the space and paint diagonally from right to left, top to bottom. Wait a moment or so before beginning in the opposite direction.

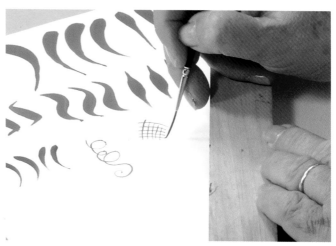

Try to space the cross lines evenly apart, again working top to bottom, but this time going diagonally from left to right.

Striping is often used around the edge of the floor of a tray, around the top or bottom edge of a coffeepot, or on a document box. There is a special striping brush for this job, and it comes in various sizes, number 1 creating the finest line, and 3 the thickest. The brush I'm using in these examples is the JoSonja's striper number 2, which has a regular paintbrush-length handle. Once you load the brush with the thin paint, the brush takes on a spoon-shaped look. Stripers for oil painting have much longer, and many more, bristles or hairs, and the handle is just a stub that fits into the palm of your hand.

The key to striping, especially around the edge of a tray, is to stand up and give yourself plenty of room to work. Have your work at a comfortable level, such as countertop height. Try placing your right foot slightly in front of your left so that you can pull the stroke from your shoulder, not just from your wrist. Rock back onto your left foot if necessary, so that you pull the stroke along the edge of the tray in one fluid motion.

Rest your little finger along the edge of the object, letting it serve as your guide to keep the entire stroke the same distance from the edge.

Keep looking ahead of your brush, not behind; in other words, watch where you are going, not where you have been. The main thing is to relax and not be tense while doing this stroke. Here again, practice, practice, and practice some more before doing any striping on an object.

Most early painted tinware and many of today's decorated objects are finished with borders. On a tray, a border is used on the flange to complement the design on the floor. Borders are painted on the top and bottom edges and around the flanges on gooseneck coffeepots and around the lid tops and front bottom edges on document boxes. You can make border designs by putting together some of the basic strokes you've learned. I am using a number 4 round brush in the following examples, but the size of the brush you use depends on the size of the object you are painting.

A series of right comma strokes makes a simple border.

A variation is to paint a right comma stroke, then a left comma stroke, alternating around the edge of the object.

A more complex variation is to first make a border of right comma strokes all around the object. Then do another round of a smaller comma stroke next to the first strokes. Next add a dot at the narrow end of each pair of comma strokes with the tip of the brush. You could add a third row of even smaller comma strokes if you want.

Another simple border can be made by using a round brush to make a series of long comma strokes along the striping line you've painted around your tray or other item.

A rickrack or zigzag border is fun to do. This is done the same way as the S stroke, but with smaller strokes and parallel to the edge of the object. Starting from the left bottom and applying very light pressure, move the brush upward on a diagonal to the right. Change directions and apply more pressure while making a diagonal stroke to the bottom right. Repeat these diagonal upward light strokes and downward heavier strokes around the object, trying to keep them uniform in length. Relax as you pull these strokes.

A variation of the elongated S stroke forms the basis of a combination of strokes that's one of my favorite borders for around the edge of an oval bread tray.

Using a round brush, begin by applying pressure as you start an S stroke. As you change directions for the ending, pull the long tail of the stroke with just the tip of the brush, applying very light pressure. Make a series of these strokes, evenly spacing them around the edge of your object where you want the border. These strokes should be about $1^1/_2$ inches long and about $^1/_4$-inch apart.

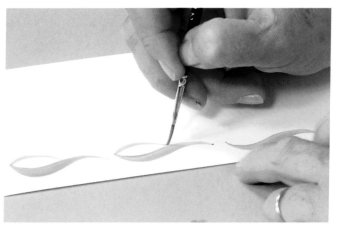

Now change to a liner brush, and pull a thin comma stroke with light pressure from the tip of each original stroke to just past the midway point on that stroke, lifting the brush as you rejoin the original stroke.

Switch back to a round brush, and pull another, thicker comma stroke to the bottom left side of each original stroke.

Apply a second, slightly smaller comma stroke to the left of each of the comma strokes you just made.

Then apply a third series of even smaller comma strokes to the left of these strokes.

Apply a second, slightly shorter comma stroke to the right of each of these strokes.

Now move to the right side of the original elongated S strokes, and apply a series of comma strokes slightly longer than the first set of comma strokes on the left side.

Finish the border pattern by applying a dot with the tip of the round brush at the bottom of each series of comma strokes.

Series of large to small comma strokes, both right and left, are often used at the ends of large trays with hand-hold cutouts.

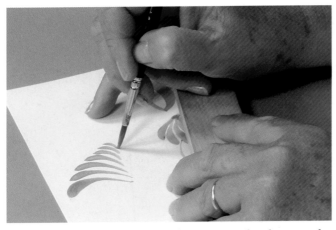

Start by marking the center of the area to be decorated. Make the largest right comma stroke slightly to the right of center, and continue making a series of comma strokes, decreasing their size as you move to the right. It is best to use an uneven number of comma strokes on each side.

Repeat the pattern to the left of center, making your left comma strokes the same sizes as those on the right.

An elaborate border pattern can be made from a combination of comma strokes, teardrops, and cross-hatching.

Begin by painting a series of elongated right comma strokes along the edge of the object with a round brush.

Make a second row and then a third row of thinner comma strokes.

Next, turn the object around so that the insides of the arches of the comma strokes are facing you, and pull a teardrop stroke between each set of three comma strokes, from about 1 to 1¹/₄ inch below the comma strokes to the top edge. Begin this stroke by applying pressure to the round brush, and release pressure as you pull the stroke, ending on the tip of the brush.

Do all the strokes in one direction, evenly spacing them; then make cross strokes in the opposite direction. This will give you better control of your spacing.

Turn your work around in the opposite direction, and use a liner brush to fill in the space under the arches of the original comma strokes with cross-hatching.

Finally, still using the liner brush, make a series of three thin comma strokes over the points where the original comma strokes meet.

Always sign and date your work after decorations have been painted. Decide on how you want your name and date to appear, and be consistent on all your future projects.

The paint must cure for about two weeks if air-drying or a minimum of forty-eight hours if using a drying oven. When the drying process is complete, erase any visible pattern lines using a pink pearl eraser. Use a tack cloth to remove any dust. Check the decorations one more time to make sure there are no smudges or excess paint to remove. If there is excess paint, sometimes a light rubbing with a moist wipe will remove acrylic paint before it has any protective coating over it. Be very careful in doing this; you do not want to rub into a good stroke and accidentally remove it.

Once any needed touch-up has been done, brush on several coats of varnish to protect the decorative painting, following the same procedure as when you sealed the base coat. Allow proper drying time between coats, and wet-sand after each.

Basic Folk-Art Flowers

Folk-art flowers are created by using combinations of the basic strokes. At first you may want to place a piece of clear acetate topped with tracing paper over the flowers shown here to practice. Once you feel comfortable with the process, practice painting them freehand. No two flowers will be identical, but they will look similar.

It's always a good idea to do some sort of practice strokes on tracing paper, shiny cardboard, newspaper, or an old telephone book to loosen up before you actually begin work on an object.

Turn your work and make a left comma stroke to form a circle, and then fill in the center to create a ball. In this example, the ball is painted vermilion or red-orange. Clean the paint from the brush; make sure all the water is out of the brush by pressing it against a paper towel.

Now paint overstrokes with a deeper shade of red.

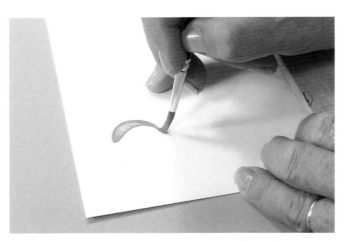

Start the rose by using a number 4 round brush to make a filled-in ball. Make a right comma stroke.

Make a series of three right comma strokes, starting from the outside right edge, with each successive stroke slightly shorter. Think of pulling these strokes from the 12 to 6 o'clock position, ending with the tails at bottom center of the ball. Clean the paint from the brush again and remove excess water.

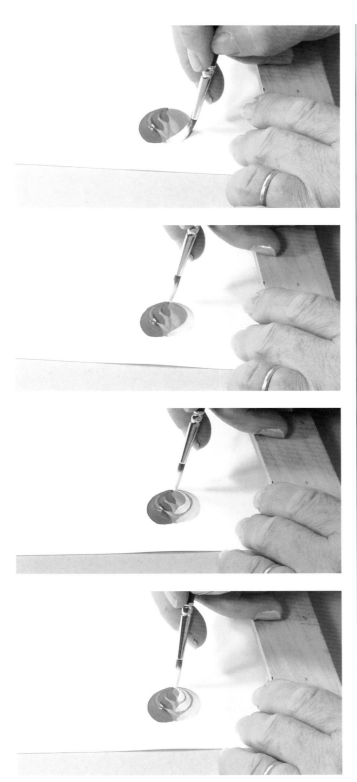

To create side petals, use the deep red to pull a series of three comma strokes to the right of the ball, each to the right of the previous stroke and slightly shorter. Adjust the position of your work and then pull three corresponding comma strokes on the left side.

Now turn your work so that the top of the ball is toward the 9 o'clock position. Using a thin white paint, apply a series of three comma strokes about the same size as the deeper red strokes, pulling them from 9 to 3 o'clock and ending at the same point on the ball as the first three overstrokes.

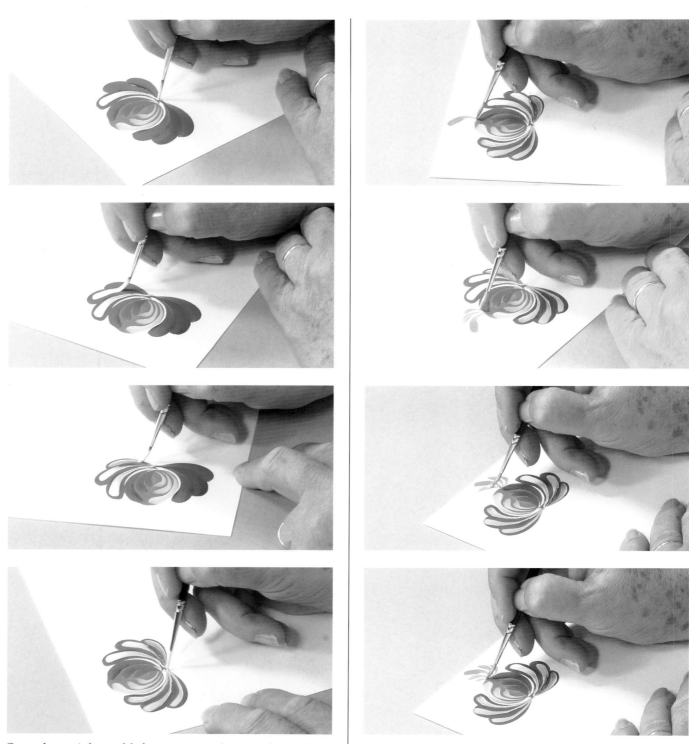

Once these right and left comma strokes are dry, either change to a number 2 round brush or use a lighter pressure to pull overstrokes on the side petals with the thin white paint. Make the overstrokes slightly shorter than the original strokes. Adjust the position of your work as you pull each overstroke.

Change to a yellow or golden color for the series of comma strokes at the top center of the flower. Use either a lighter pressure or a smaller round or liner brush, adjusting the position of your work as you pull each stroke.

Use green paint and a liner brush to make the stem. Pull a slightly curved stem from the bottom center of the ball downward, using the tip of the brush and releasing pressure as you go.

Switching back to a number 4 round brush, make comma strokes with the green paint to form leaves.

Use left comma strokes for the right-side leaves and vice versa.

Reposition your work as you paint the leaves on both sides.

To finish the design, use a liner brush to make a few small right comma strokes with yellow paint at the bottom of the design.

And finally, make a squiggle up the stem with thin yellow or golden paint.

To add details to the flower, use the number 5 round brush to pull three right comma strokes in medium or pinkish red from right to left across the ball. Position your work to pull the first stroke from 12 to 6 o'clock, and adjust the work slightly as you pull each of the other strokes.

This rose also begins with a ball, this time red.

Now add white paint to your brush to create a lighter shade of pink, or you could use a clean brush with the white paint alone. Pull three left comma strokes from the left to right, with the first from 9 to 3 o'clock and adjusting the position of your work for each stroke. The thin tails should end either slightly underneath or above the corresponding right comma stroke. Which-ever way you choose, be consistent with all the strokes.

Decorate the top of the rose using a number 2 round brush and thin white paint. First make a small left comma stroke.

Then make a circle from several dots. Often painters start with large dots and make them gradually smaller to form the circle.

Using the liner brush with either the lighter pink or white paint, make two thin vertical comma strokes over the lighter side, positioning your work to pull these from 9 to 3 o'clock.

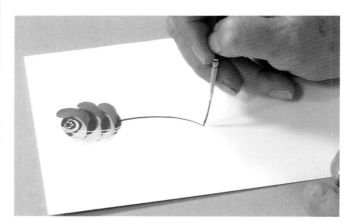

Changing the position of the work so that the bottom of the flower is toward you, use the number 2 liner brush with thin green paint to pull the stem of the flower curving to the left, from 12 to 6 o'clock, using light pressure on the tip of the brush.

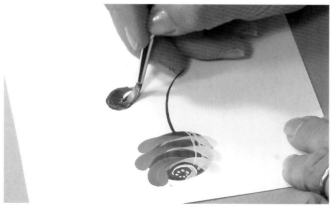

Then with the number 5 round brush, pull two short comma strokes, one right and one left, to form an oval for each leaf with a lighter green paint.

It's best to use an uneven number of leaves, such as three on one side of the stem and two on the other.

Once all of the ovals are formed, use the number 2 liner brush and the same thin green paint you used for the stem to create a vein and stem for each leaf. Begin the vein slightly down from the tip of each leaf, and follow through with the stroke to make the stem.

Then touch the tip of the liner brush at an angle all around the leaves to create the appearance of toothed edges.

Now with a number 2 round brush, pull a few comma strokes on each side of the stem above the oval leaves and a few to the left of the farthest left leaf stem. Adjust your work as necessary to pull these strokes properly.

Add decorative touches to the design with thin yellow paint and a number 2 liner brush, making three short comma strokes across the stem just beneath the flower.

Make three more comma strokes at the bottom of the design, below the stems and leaves, and end with a series of squiggles starting at the bottom of the stem, coming about halfway up, and going out the right side of the design.

Now load the number 5 round brush with a lighter yellow or even white to form the petals from short comma strokes. Not all will be of the same length or size, but it's best to use an uneven number. Eleven flower petals usually works well. Decide where you want your first petal, position the brush for a comma stroke, apply pressure, and pull toward flower center.

To make a daisy, begin by creating the flower center, using the tip of a number 5 round brush and gold oxide paint to dab a small oval.

Pull the second petal diagonally across from the first one.

Fill in with comma strokes for all the other petals. Some will be more curved, and a few others, especially at bottom center, may be somewhat straight. For variety, you can begin a few petals with the tip of the brush, then apply pressure before pulling the stroke.

Then, with a fine liner brush and a contrasting color such as red, pull fine lines from the center out about halfway onto the individual petals. Do not pull all the exact same way; vary the strokes, making some thinner and lighter and others darker and heavier. Make some shorter or longer, and one line may branch off another line.

Add random dots of several different colors, such as red, black, gold oxide and brown, around the flower center with the tip of the liner brush. Place more dots around the bottom of the flower center and fewer dots around the top.

Now use a number 2 liner brush with thin green paint to pull a slightly curved stem.

Each of the two leaves is made with three strokes, using a number 5 round brush and green paint. Begin with the center stroke of the left leaf. Touching just the tip of the round brush to the surface, slightly pull and apply pressure, and then begin to release pressure as you continue to pull this variation of the comma stroke toward the bottom of the stem.

Add an elongated right comma stroke to the right side of this stroke.

Add another elongated right comma stroke to the left side of the first stroke.

Then make a series of small comma strokes across each leaf vein.

Repeat with three elongated left comma strokes on the other side of the stem to form the right leaf.

Add decorative touches to the design with golden paint and a number 2 liner brush. Make a squiggle over the stem and going out the right side of the design.

With a liner brush and a thin darker green paint, such as pine green or even Hooker's green, make a thin vein down the center of each leaf, pulling from the outside edge toward the stem.

Then make three short comma strokes at the bottom of the leaves.

Once all five petals are completed, use a contrasting color and the tip of the number 5 round brush to dab in the flower center.

Using this same color, thin the paint and pull some strokes with a liner brush to indicate veins in the petals. Work from the center outward about two-thirds of the way, following the curve of the petals.

Begin a five-petal flower by deciding on your center point and making five petals around it, each consisting of a short right and left comma stroke. It's best to start your first petal slightly to the left of top center, then make another petal on either side of the first, and finish with the bottom two petals. Turn your work as you progress around the flower.

You may also add some dots around the flower center in both colors with the point of the liner brush.

Using thin green paint and the liner brush, pull the stem, curving it slightly.

Now, using a darker green and the liner brush, pull veins in the leaves from stem to tip.

Then place the round brush on the stem where you want to start a leaf; apply pressure, wiggling the brush as you pull and release pressure, ending on the tip of the brush. You will need to pull at least two of these strokes next to each other to form the full leaf. If you prefer a fatter leaf, or if the strokes don't meet in the center, pull a third stroke between the first two.

You may also make some short comma strokes across the center veins.

Decorate the design with a squiggle over the stem.

Using the tip of the round brush, dab in the flower center.

With a slightly darker shade of thin paint and the liner brush, outline each petal, starting from the left side of the petal where it touches the center, and pulling the stroke up and around toward the top of the petal.

Begin a dogwood flower by determining your flower center position and making four petals around it. Each petal consists of a right and left comma stroke, with one to three shorter strokes in between. Start with the top petal slightly to the right of top center. Using a number 5 round brush, make a short right comma stroke, then a left comma stroke. Fill in between these two comma strokes with one or more slightly shorter strokes. Next, do the petal directly opposite the one you just completed, starting with the bottom stroke. Then do the right petal and finally the left petal, making them all as close in size as possible to the first.

As you reach the tip of the petal, apply slight pressure to the brush as you outline the indentation. Gradually release pressure as you continue pulling the stroke around the remainder of the petal. Do this for all four petals.

With a color that's darker or contrasts with your flower petals, pull some veins in each petal, beginning from the flower center and working outward, following the curve of the petal. Pull these veins out about three-quarters of the length of the petals.

Use the tip of the liner brush to apply an uneven number of yellow dots around the center of the flower, starting at the base of the left petal and circling across the bases of the lower and right petals. You can begin with larger dots, gradually decreasing in size as you go around the flower center.

Now make a slightly curving stem using the liner brush and green paint.

Each leaf is made from a right and left comma stroke, using green paint and a round brush.

Again, an uneven number of leaves is preferable.

Then, using thin gold oxide paint and the liner brush, pull leaf stems and veins, starting from the stem and working outward toward the leaf and into the leaf vein.

To vary your flower compositions, you could use the gold oxide for additional details on the leaf or shadow on the stems.

To give leaves the effect of turned-up edges, use the liner brush with thin gold oxide. Pull a thin comma stroke on one edge of a leaf, beginning at the tip and working back about two-thirds of the length of the leaf.

Add decorative touches to your design with the liner brush and yellow or golden paint. Make three short comma strokes on the stem near the flower.

Make three more comma strokes at the bottom end of the stem.

Paint a squiggle across the stem and going out to the right side.

To add the right-side petal, turn the work sideways so that you can pull this stroke from 9 to 3 o'clock, working from the bottom of the flower. Apply pressure at the tulip base, and as you pull the petal, gradually release the pressure on the brush as you flare outward, ending on the brush tip.

Turn the flower upside down so that you can pull the other petal from 12 to 6 o'clock. Apply pressure as you begin the stroke, and release pressure as you pull up and flare outward.

Begin the tulip by making a right and left comma stroke with the number 5 round brush, and fill in the center with the teardrop stroke. Turn your work so that you can pull the strokes properly.

Turn your work again and use the liner brush and thin green paint to pull a slightly curving stem.

You could also highlight this pointed leaf with a contrasting color to add more interest. Apply a thin comma stroke along the upper edge of the leaf with the liner brush.

The leaves are made from a series of comma strokes of varying lengths, using the number 5 round brush. To vary the style of leaves, you could create a pointed one by beginning on the brush tip, applying pressure as you start to pull the stroke, and releasing pressure as you get to the end.

Now using a number 2 round brush, add details to the tulip with a contrasting color. Starting at the outer edge of each petal, apply pressure and pull a comma stroke down to the point where the petal and flower center meet.

Add a few more comma strokes to the right and left of the flower center.

Then, using the tip of the number 2 round brush with green paint to correspond to the stem line, add a dab of paint at the point where the stem and flower meet.

Using white paint, make an uneven number of over-strokes in varying lengths on the tulip center.

Add a few contrasting short comma strokes with the number 2 round brush to both ends of the stem. If you wish, you can add a squiggle as done for the earlier flowers.

Then pull three comma strokes on the opposite side from 9 to 3 o'clock. Turn your work for each stroke as necessary.

Change to a fine liner brush and make diagonal strokes from upper right to lower left for cross-hatching.

Begin this flower with a number 5 round brush and the color of your choice, making a comma stroke from 12 to 6 o'clock. Make two additional strokes to the right of the first one, each slightly shorter.

Wait a moment for the paint to dry, and then do the second set of diagonal strokes from upper left to lower right. You can make the diagonal lines either straight or slightly curved. In the example in the photos, they are slightly curved. Clean the brush and remove any excess water. If using oils, swish the brush in turpentine or mineral spirits and blot dry on a paper towel.

Now load the fine liner brush with a contrasting color such as yellow to pull a fine stroke along the inside edges of the center comma strokes.

Turn your work to begin at the base of each stroke. Follow the inside curve, pull the stroke upward, and extend it past the end of the comma stroke, ending by flaring the fine line outward at the top. Clean the brush again.

Load the fine liner brush with green for the stem, and pull the stem downward in a slightly curved line.

This time using the number 5 round brush loaded with green, make a series of comma strokes of various lengths and thicknesses, applying more or less pressure on the brush, to form the leaves.

You can make an overstroke of a yellow comma stroke along the upper edge of one of the larger leaves to add variety.

You may also want to include some smaller comma strokes in a contrasting color as leaves, made with light pressure on your number 2 round brush or a liner brush.

Add three small comma strokes at the bottom of the stem.

With the number 4 round brush and a contrasting color such as yellow, make a series of three comma strokes above the opening at the flower's top center.

Finish by using the fine liner brush to make a squiggle over the stem and going off to the right.

Add a set of three comma strokes extending out from between the second and third comma strokes on each side.

Small Round Tray with Black Background

Before beginning any project, prepare your tin as described earlier in the book. This design on a small round tray that has been base-coated black uses several of the basic brush strokes you've learned. This first project will include all the details about applying your pattern, as well as some general information, which will be the same for all projects. As you work through the other projects, refer back to this section as necessary. The more you paint, the more familiar and comfortable you will become with the process. Often when working a design for the first time, or if you want to have a permanent record of the pattern and completed design, it's best to do a trial run on shiny black cardboard before painting it on your tin piece.

Begin by tracing the design of three ball flowers and
leaves onto tracing paper. Then transfer the pattern
tracing onto the black cardboard or tin item.

Start by centering your pattern where you want it placed on your painting surface, and insert a piece of graphite paper between the pattern and painting surface. Secure the paper to the tin with small magnets. Once the pattern is in place, use a stylus to mark the circles for the ball flowers and leaves only. Do not indicate the overstrokes. After you are familiar with the painting strokes, you probably will need to indicate the leaves and other strokes with only a line down the center of the strokes. But you need to practice and become familiar with your painting before just indicating with simple lines where strokes should be.

Now use your tack cloth to remove any lint or dust.

Whenever you need to add a medium to your paint, such as Flow Medium or Magic Mix for ease in pulling strokes, please do so. I prefer to just tip my brush into the medium or brush mix, rather than add it to my paint on the palette. But each painter has his or her own preference, so do what is comfortable for you. Additionally, whenever you feel the need to remove any excess paint from your brush, clean the brush before continuing. Only you will know how to keep your brushes doing the best work for you.

Begin the painting process by filling in the three ball flowers with a number 4 round brush and paint color of your choice. Here I've used vermilion. Use a wooden bridge to keep your wrist elevated off the painting surface, and use your little finger to steady your hand. Depending on the paint coverage, the ball flowers may need a second coat, but make sure the first coat is completely dry to the touch before applying more paint.

Using a number 2 liner brush and green oxide, pull curved stems on each of the three ball flowers.

Next do the cross-hatching down the center of each ball flower, using thin white paint in the fine liner brush. Use either all straight or all slightly curved lines for the cross-hatching.

The strokes all end at the bottom center, where the stem joins the ball flower. Do all the right sides before going to the left. On the right sides, pull the strokes from 12 to 6 o'clock. On the left side, pull from 9 to 3 o'clock.

Switch back to the number 4 round brush to begin the overstrokes on the ball flowers. You could use naphthol crimson, burgundy, or permanent alizarin for the first overstrokes. There are three comma strokes on each side, beginning with the outside edge and working toward the center.

The leaves are made with several comma strokes placed side by side, using green oxide in the number 4 round brush. On the left side of the stem, pull the largest comma stroke for the center of the leaf; then pull a shorter comma stroke on either side of the first stroke.

The leaf on the right side is made of four comma strokes side by side, beginning with the longest stroke at the top and working down.

For the leaves at the bottom, the two outside strokes are pulled from the bottom up toward the stem, and the center is pulled from the end of the stem down.

For the other stroke, tip the brush to the surface, apply pressure as you are pulling downward, and flare out.

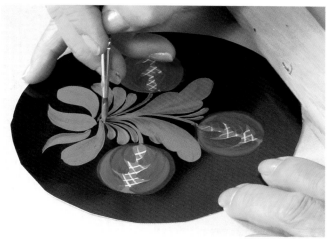

You can then pull a few single comma strokes with the number 4 round brush in green and yellow to fill in the empty spaces. You may want to change to a number 2 liner brush for some of the smaller comma strokes, especially those up near the ball flowers.

By now the overstrokes on the ball flowers should be dry to the touch. Using a number 2 round brush with thin white paint, pull a smaller comma stroke over each of the red overstrokes.

With the number 2 round brush and yellow paint, pull a series of comma strokes from the top center of each ball flower.

At this point, the green leaves should be dry, so you can add some decorative strokes on them. Using a number 2 liner brush with yellow paint, outline the larger comma strokes.

To add veins and other detail lines, start from the stem end of the leaf and work toward the tip, pulling a few lines.

Paint three small comma strokes just below each ball flower.

To add some interest and detail to the design, pull thin yellow lines on the upper side of the right and left stems and to the left side of the center stem.

With the number 2 round brush, add some white dot flowers in the empty spaces near the ends of the larger leaves. Begin with the center dot, and encircle it with five more dots. Use an uneven number of dot flowers in your design.

Add some yellow dots along the center edge of the right leaf, beginning at the bottom with the largest dots, and getting smaller as you work upward.

Finish with a few squiggles, using thin yellow paint and the fine liner brush. Have fun and relax when doing these finishing touches.

If your project is completed on a tin piece, it is now ready to cure, clean by removing any pattern lines, and varnish to preserve the details.

Small Round Tray with Red Background

This design is similar to that in the first project, yet differs somewhat.

Begin by filling in the center solid ball flower with yellow oxide using a number 4 round brush. The two outside flowers have the base color showing through the cross-hatching, so you need to do the cross-hatching first on those flowers. Use a number 2 script liner. There is also cross-hatching in the space between the stems. Whether you use straight or curved lines for your cross-hatching, follow through so that all are the same.

By this time, the center ball flower should be dry and ready for the overstrokes. Leaving the yellow oxide in your brush, referred to as a dirty brush, dip it into the white; then mix the colors slightly on palette paper. This gives you a lighter shade of yellow oxide to pull four comma strokes about two-thirds to three-quarters of the way across the ball flower. Have your work turned so that you pull these strokes from 9 to 3 o'clock.

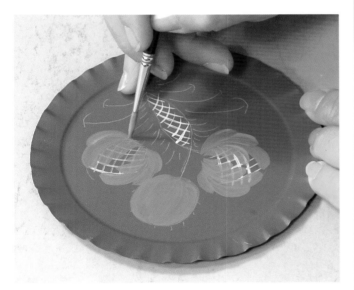

Once the cross-hatching is dry on the flowers, use a number 4 round brush with yellow oxide to pull the comma strokes on both sides of the left and right flowers.

Still using a dirty brush, dip the round brush into white again, which will lighten the paint in your brush even more. Now make another, shorter comma stroke over each of the previous strokes on the two outside ball flowers.

Add more white paint to your brush, and pull comma strokes from right to left on the center ball flower, working from 12 to 6 o'clock. You can pull the tails of these comma strokes on top of or under the tails of the left side strokes; just be sure to do all the same. Then add a small comma stroke at the top of this flower, and pull two curved line strokes down the left side with a number 2 round brush. Add a circle of dots inside the curve of the small comma stroke.

With the number 4 round brush and green oxide paint, pull three full comma strokes beside one another on each side of the stem lines, but not into the cross-hatching.

Now pull the stems with the same paint and a number 2 script liner brush. For interest, you may want to tip the line brush that has green oxide into white paint to make a slightly lighter shade of green.

Outline these larger comma stroke leaves with yellow and the number 2 script liner brush.

Then pull a few fine lines from the stem end outward to add more interest to the design.

With a number 2 round brush and yellow oxide, pull various size comma strokes on the right side of the right stem. You could tip the brush into white for the first strokes at the top, and gradually tip it into green the farther down you pull strokes, and then add more green for the comma strokes on the left side of the left stem. Using this dirty brush technique varies the shades of the strokes.

Now, using a number 2 liner brush, add a few small green comma strokes at the bottom, a dab of green paint where each stem joins the flower, and three short comma strokes on the stem.

To further decorate the two outside flowers, use the number 2 liner to add a few white comma strokes at the top. They can face downward or toward the center.

With a number 2 script liner and thin yellow paint, make a few decorative squiggles in the empty space.

Finish off the design with a simple comma stroke border using a number 3 round brush.

Oblong Candle-Snuffer Tray

This design is taken from a large, round antique tin spice container in our collection. It consists of three simple ball flowers and a variety of comma strokes. Note that when transferring the design, I only used a line through the center of each comma stroke to indicate the placement; I did not outline each stroke.

Begin by using a number 5 round brush to fill in the ball flowers with naphthol crimson.

When the paint is dry, make darker red overstrokes, using a number 3 round brush and permanent alizarin. It is somewhat hard to see the difference between the shades of red in the photos. Turn your work to pull these strokes from 12 to 6 o'clock.

Next add white comma strokes, also using the number 3 round brush. Also add the white dot to the middle ball flower.

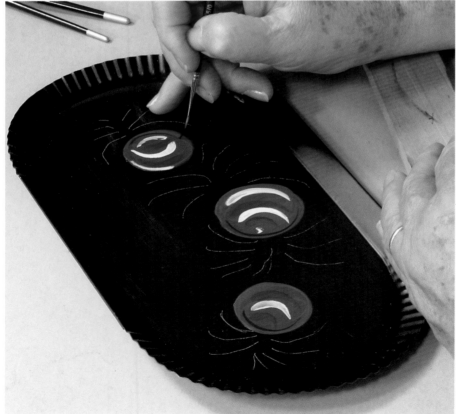

Change to thin black paint and a 5/0 liner brush, and pull a thin stroke at the top of each ball flower.

Now use the number 4 round brush with green oxide paint to pull all the green comma strokes.

Complete all the yellow comma strokes with Turner's yellow and the number 4 round brush for large strokes and the number 2 round brush for smaller strokes.

Then use a number 2 striper brush with thin Turner's yellow to paint a stripe around the outer edge of the tray floor. To keep the stripe an even distance from the edge, use your little finger as a guide, running it along the outside edge of the tray as you paint.

Red Wall Match Safe

The design on this red wall match safe should look familiar—the flower is the comma-stroke flower with cross-hatched center (page 73), and the bottom border is the elaborate one at the end of the borders section (page 48).

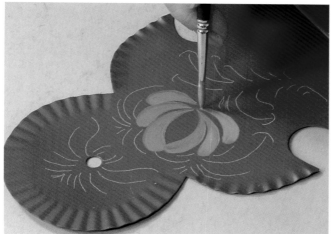

Begin by painting the comma stroke flower with the number 5 round brush and yellow oxide paint.

With the number 4 round brush and thin white paint, do the overstrokes on the flower.

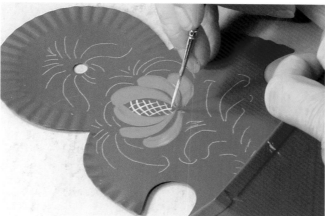

Next use the number 2 script liner brush with thin white paint to do the cross-hatching.

Then use the number 4 round brush with green oxide to make all the green comma-stroke leaves.

Again using the liner brush, pull the stem from the base to the bottom of the flower, applying pressure when you begin the stroke.

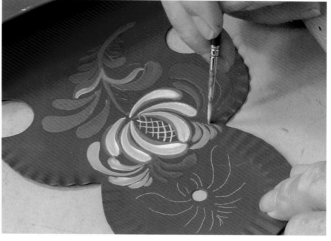

Using a smaller number 2 round brush and yellow oxide, paint all the yellow details plus the yellow comma-stroke leaves.

Continue with the yellow detail work around the top of the match safe.

Then fill in the cross-hatching with thin white paint and the number 2 script liner brush.

For the bottom border design, use a number 3 round brush and the yellow oxide to paint the first row of the swag.

Proceed to do the remaining two rows of swags using a number 2 round brush. Finish with the two teardrop strokes and two sets of small swags over the teardrop strokes.

Teapot Design

This design is from a teapot I painted several years ago, shown in the reproduction gallery section of this book (page 134). In this demonstration, I'm painting the design on the shiny black cardboard.

Starting with vermilion paint in your number 5 round brush, fill in the ball flower and three buds.

Change to green oxide paint in the number 5 round brush, and complete all the green leaves. Do not paint the green overstroke on the flower at this point.

Once the ball flower is dry to the touch, you can begin the overstrokes on the flower. With the number 5 round brush and either permanent alizarin or burgundy, pull a comma stroke from the center bottom around the right side.

Turn the work to pull another comma stroke on the other side, using the number 5 round brush with Turner's yellow paint.

Using Turner's yellow and a 5/0 fine liner, do the cross-hatching in the center of the flower.

With the number 2 liner brush and darker red paint of your choice, form a circle with two comma strokes to indicate the top opening of the ball flower.

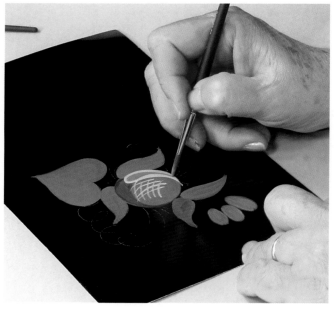

Switch to the number 4 round brush with green oxide, and pull a smaller comma stroke over the yellow stroke.

With green in the number 2 liner brush again, pull a few short lines from the green overstroke.

Using the number 2 liner brush with yellow, add the details on the leaves, contining into a curlicue off the tip of the left leaf.

Add a few vein lines on each half of the heart-shaped leaf.

Pull a yellow comma stroke from the top to bottom on the heart-shaped leaf.

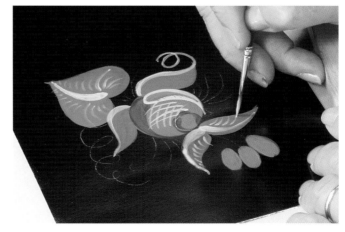

Add the remaining yellow details and the vein lines to the top two leaves.

With green in the number 2 liner brush, pull the green strokes on each side of the buds.

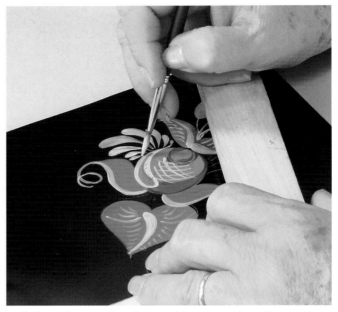

Switch to the number 3 round brush with yellow paint, and pull the series of comma strokes on the upper left side, turning your work as necessary.

Change to thin yellow, and add the stems to the buds.

Then pull the comma strokes on the right side and bottom.

Make curlicues on the right side with the 5/0 liner brush and thin yellow paint.

If you're using this design on a teapot, make a series of yellow teardrop strokes with the number 3 round brush under the teapot handle.

Add two small comma strokes in the centers of the two larger curlicues.

Groupings of elongated comma strokes are on the teapot lid around the knob.

A border of zigzag or rickrack strokes is painted with a number 2 flat brush around the top outer edge of the teapot.

One-Sheet Waiter Tray

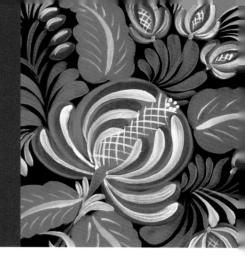

This design for a traditional one-sheet waiter that has been base-coated black uses many of the strokes that you have practiced. Though I drew lines only where comma strokes are placed, I did outline the placement of the four large leaves, as well as the central flower and buds.

Begin by using a number 4 round brush with vermilion to fill in all the buds and the central flower.

Change to green oxide in the number 4 round brush, and pull the strokes for the large leaves. Start with the tip of the leaf, pulling that comma stroke down through the middle of the leaf. Then do either all the right-hand or left-hand strokes, pulling them down to the base of the leaf. It doesn't matter which side you do first, but finish one side before starting on the other. Once the large leaves are completed, switch to the number 2 liner brush and add the stems, pulling from bottom to top, releasing pressure as you come to the top end of the stem. Also pull all the individual green comma strokes throughout the design.

Using the number 4 round brush and naphthol crimson, begin the overstroke painting on the central flower and buds. Starting on the right outside or largest comma stroke, work toward the inside or smallest stroke, ending each of these strokes at the bottom center of this flower.

With the 5/0 liner brush and thin white paint, do the cross-hatching in the center of the flower.

Wait a moment for the paint to dry; then do the opposite direction of cross-hatching.

Add a few dots in a circle at the top of the cross-hatching.

Using a number 3 round brush and thin or transparent white paint, add the white overstrokes to the center flower.

Use a number 2 round brush to add the red overstroke details to the buds.

The cross-hatching strokes on the buds can also be completed with a 5/0 liner at this time.

Next, with the number 2 round brush, complete the balance of the thin or transparent white over-strokes on the buds and on the four comma strokes at the base of the center flower.

Add the short green stroke at the base of the flower to connect it to the stem. Also add a circle of dots at the top of each bud to correspond with those on the center flower.

Now with a number 2 liner brush and Turner's yellow, add the center vein lines on the leaves, starting at the base of each leaf, and releasing pressure as you pull in a curved line toward the tip.

With a number 2 script liner brush and Turner's yellow, pull short, curved outer vein lines on the leaves, from just off center outward.

Switch back to the number 3 round brush with Turner's yellow, and complete the remainder of the comma strokes in the design.

Also place a dab of Turner's yellow at the base of each
bud where it meets the stem.

To make the border, you will stripe the edges of the tray floor, but create a semicircle at each cut-corner edge. First you need to make a template of the semicircle so that all will be the same size. I use a Jumbo Circles template and a piece of cardstock.

Once the paper template is made to the size you need, place it in each cut corner and use a chalk pencil to lightly trace around the pattern.

I prefer to stripe the straight edges first, then go to the semicircles, but do whatever makes you feel more comfortable. Use a number 2 striper with thin Turner's yellow paint, and with your little finger as a guide, follow along the outer edge of the tray to keep the stripe as straight as possible.

Then do the four semicircles on the cut-corner edges.

Add lines of the rickrack stroke along the four cut
corners, using a number 2 flat brush and Turner's
yellow paint.

The border on the flange of the tray can be just comma strokes as shown here, or you may elaborate more. Starting with the two short ends, use a number 4 round brush to make five strokes across each end. Next do the long sides, making eight strokes on each side. Finally, do the four cut-corner ends, with three strokes on each of those sections. However you choose to decorate the flange, be consistent with the number of strokes on each like section.

Two-Sheet Waiter Tray

T his is a fun project that uses many of the basic steps you have learned and includes lots of details. Do not be intimidated by the details, but relax as you work through the design.

Begin by filling in all the red areas. Using the number 4 round brush with naphthol crimson, paint the stroke flower on the left, the solid center with stroke petals on the right, the two large buds at the top, and the three smaller buds on the right and left side. Pull the red stem lines with the number 2 liner brush.

Next, with the number 4 round brush and green oxide, complete the two solid green leaves at the bottom and all the green comma strokes and details.

Then do the cross-hatching on the open-center flower, with double straight lines done in thin white paint with the 5/0 fine liner.

Paint a yellow dot in the center of each open diamond in the cross-hatching.

Using the number 4 round brush with either alizarin crimson or burgundy, do all the dark red overstrokes, including those on the buds.

While you're waiting for the overstrokes to dry, begin the yellow stroke work, using a number 2 script liner brush and Turner's yellow to pull curved center vein lines on the two large green leaves.

Then pull the small vein lines on the two leaves.

Complete the remaining comma-stroke details in the design using the number 3 round brush with the same yellow paint. Use a number 2 round brush for some of the smaller comma strokes.

Paint all the fine cross-hatching down the center of the design, between the red stems and at the stem end of the large flower between the stem and the yellow comma strokes.

When your red overstrokes are dry, begin the transparent or thin white paint overstrokes with a number 3 round brush on the flowers and buds. Make these white overstrokes slightly smaller than the red ones. Pay attention to the design so that you begin each stroke at the proper location; most of them begin at the top of the flower, but some begin at the stem end.

With the number 2 script liner and thin white paint, outline a few of the white strokes as shown in the design. Also paint a thin white stroke between each of the comma strokes on the solid red flower.

Add white dots over the elongated white comma strokes in the center of the open comma-stroke flower, as well as along the inside edges of the white strokes on the buds.

Now use the number 2 script liner brush to paint a series of fine yellow lines over the clusters of green comma strokes throughout the design.

Continue to use the number 2 script liner brush with thin yellow paint to complete the many curlicues or squiggles in the design. Relax and work your brush in a continuous circular motion, making some circles larger than others.

Striping is next. Make a template for the corners as described for the One-Sheet Waiter Tray. This time I decided on a shallower curve. Again, I prefer to stripe the straight sides before doing the semicircles, but do whatever feels best to you.

The flange has a cluster of strokes painted at the center of each end, each cut corner, and each half of both long sides. For each cluster, begin by pulling a straight or teardrop stroke at the center, beginning at the base of the flange and working toward the top edge. Next make either all the right or all the left strokes. If you begin with the first stroke to one side of center, and pull that one stroke for each cluster all the way around the tray, this will help you keep them similar in length and shape. Repeat this process until you have all four strokes on the same side of center at each location all the way around the tray. Then go back and start the strokes on the opposite side of center, working all the way around the tray for each stroke, until all are completed. If you prefer to do all the strokes of one cluster at the same time, that is fine as well. Do what works best for you.

Gallery of Reproduction Painted Tinware

The pieces in this section are all reproduction pieces, most of them made by Ray and decorated by me. A few are old pieces that we restored. They are painted in acrylic unless otherwise noted. I enjoy painting the old designs, whether it is by creating my own patterns from existing pieces that I have seen and examined closely or by copying patterns that I have acquired.

Above: *This one-sheet waiter with black background has two yellow birds with brown wings, red strawberries, green and yellow comma-stroke leaves, and white details. Yellow striping is on the edge of the tray floor, and yellow comma strokes are on the flange.*

133

I borrowed this design from a tray that sold at auction in March 2006. The red one-sheet waiter has an opaque white band around the floor, orange and vermilion flowers with yellow accents, vermilion berries, and green leaves. All have black details, with black dots and squiggly lines filling in the spaces. A yellow stripe is on each edge of the white band, and a single row of yellow comma strokes is on the flange.

This black teapot has a vermilion central ball flower and buds with alizarin crimson, green, and yellow details. The leaves are green with yellow veins, and there are yellow filler strokes and large squiggles. A yellow rickrack border is around the top edge. In the next view, you can see the comma-stroke details on the lid. I created this design from several pictures taken while on vacation several years ago, and it is included in the project section (page 101).

I borrowed an original at Merritt's Antiques to design my pattern for this black gooseneck coffeepot. It has a white band along the bottom with a design of vermilion flowers, buds, and berries, alizarin crimson details, and semitransparent green leaves. All the flowers and leaves have blackline work details. The design above the white band is completed in yellow for the flowers, leaves, and comma strokes, with vermilion finger-painted highlights and black details. The flange has a triple stripe—a broad stripe around the center, with a fine stripe on each side of that. The dome lid has a single row of comma strokes around the edge, with starburst-effect comma strokes radiating from the brass knob.

This gooseneck coffeepot has a black background with a white shield inset. The semitransparent design in brown, vermilion, and blue is outlined in black and has black details. Yellow comma strokes enhance the top edge, lower edge of the shield, bottom flange, handle, gore beneath the handle, and dome lid. I purchased this pattern from HSEAD in the mid-1990s.

I created this design from a coffeepot recently sold at auction; we were permitted to photograph it during the auction preview. The black gooseneck coffeepot has white bands at both top and bottom with stroke-work designs in semitransparent green, vermilion, and yellow, all with black details. The strokework design above the bottom band is done all in yellow, with yellow comma strokes and stripes completing the details. Note the comma-stroke details on the dome lid also.

Painted in oils, this straight-spout coffeepot with black background has a semitransparent white circle on each side, with vermilion and yellow floral elements and green leaves. Black details complete the design. Yellow comma strokes are around the circle and edge of the lid. Around the upper edge of the coffeepot is a yellow scalloped band with black details. In the second view, you can see the details of the lid.

This red side-spout coffeepot has a yellow bird with green wing, vermilion ball flowers with alizarin crimson and white stroke details, three large green leaves with yellow veins, and green and yellow fill-in stroke leaves. There is a yellow stripe along the bottom and a row of comma strokes along the top edge. In the next view, you can see the cluster of strokework beneath the spout and handle, as well as the details of the lid. This piece also has a light antiquing. I adapted the design from a combination of elements from several other designs.

Miniatures are fun to make and decorate. The design for this miniature red apple dish was created from a full-size pattern. It is painted in yellow with black details. There are two views to help you visualize the shape.

This miniature coffeepot is a copy of one we made for the 2005 Pennsylvania Tree–Christmas Pageant of Peace in Washington, D.C. Each of the fifty artisans from the Reading-Berks Chapter of the Pennsylvania Guild of Craftsmen made three identical ornaments. Ray made my coffeepots, and I decorated them with a typical Pennsylvania Dutch design that I adapted from a full-size design. The first was enclosed in a two-piece plastic globe for the Washington, D.C., tree and was retained by the pageant. The second was displayed on a tree in the Pennsylvania State Capitol and now is in a permanent display. This, the third coffeepot of our series, was displayed in the Reading Public Museum in Pennsylvania and later returned to us. COLLECTION OF RAY AND PAT OXENFORD

The early tinsmiths probably used their tin scraps for miniatures and toys so that they would have less waste of materials. The smaller pieces required for these items could easily be cut from the leftovers from making larger objects. This Santa and pig toy was Ray's first tin item, and it whet his appetite to acquire tinsmithing tools and begin learning the art. When Dawson and Mary Gilespy, reproduction tin toymakers of Oley, Pennsylvania, were thinking about retiring, they contacted Ray to come work with Dawson in his workshop. This is the toy that Ray created during that session. I was given the blank tin toy without any picture or seeing how Mary painted it. "Santa's Midnight Flyer" is our finished toy. COLLECTION OF RAY AND PAT OXENFORD

The design for this oval bun tray was adapted from an old pattern. It is a restored piece. In the first view, the flowers and buds have a white base with red, blue, and black details. Leaves are green with yellow details and yellow filler strokes. There are yellow stripes and comma-stroke details along with rickrack strokes over the end handhold areas, and comma strokes surround the outside upper edge. COLLECTION OF RAY AND PAT OXENFORD

Here is another restored old piece, a balance-scale pan. Typically these were not decorated, but I combined elements from other patterns to paint this design. The flower has a white base with red and black details, and the two large leaves are yellow with black details. The border is the same as that on the restored oval bun tray, along with a simple comma-stroke border around the upper edge of the outside. COLLECTION OF RAY AND PAT OXENFORD

These two hinged-lid canisters were restored for a client.
Both have designs going completely around, and the larger
one also has a white band around the top edge. The flowers
have a vermilion base with red and semitransparent white
overstrokes. Leaves and stroke leaves are green and yellow.
The lids have yellow comma strokes around the edge and
elongated strokes in a geometric pattern on top.

COLLECTION OF MARYANN SMITH-DISNEY

Gallery of Early Painted Tinware

To get a better understanding of the early tinware, it is best to study actual items. I've been fortunate to be able to look closely at many pieces over the years to study their designs and try to determine how they were painted. Because my husband was in the antique business for more than forty-five years, many excellent examples of tinware were readily available for me to copy the designs. Recently I also had the privilege of examining an entire private collection to share with you for this book.

Above: This half-sheet waiter with black background has a white border on the floor of the tray. Vermilion and green are the primary design colors, with black details. A thin yellow stripe outlines the inside edge of the floor band. Yellow comma strokes complement the flange. LANDIS VALLEY MUSEUM COLLECTION

141

The early sheets of tin measured only 10 x 14 inches. A one-sheet waiter or two half-sheet waiters could be made from one sheet of tin. If a larger waiter was desired, two sheets of tin were seamed together to make a two-sheet waiter.

This half-sheet waiter measures $8^3/_4$ x $6^1/_2$ inches. The background color is red, with four large leaves of medium green in the center that have dark green and white comma-stroke details. The details on the right and left leaves are no longer visible. Each leaf is outlined in fine yellow linework, with squiggles and cross-hatching in the center. The tray has a yellow stripe around the floor and a simple teardrop stroke on the flange. PRIVATE COLLECTION

Comma strokes enhance the flange of this half-sheet waiter. Measuring $8^3/_4$ x 6 inches, it has a black background, with a semitransparent white border around the edge of the floor. The design is in red and green with black detail work. A yellow stripe borders the inside edge of the white band, and there is a finer yellow stripe on the lower edge of the flange.

PRIVATE COLLECTION

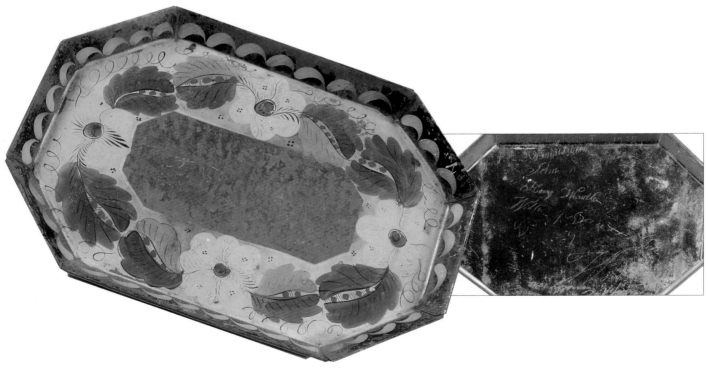

This one-sheet waiter measuring 12 1/4 x 8 3/4 inches has an asphaltum background with a 1 3/4-inch semi-transparent white border and a crystallized center on the tray floor. The design is double-circle ball flowers in vermilion, with yellow finger-painted details on the right half and three yellow strokes on the left side of the flowers. The double ball flowers have elegant fine-line black detail strokes. Leaves are yellow and green, with red berries and black detail. Some of the yellow leaves are painted over the crystallized center. Black squiggles and dots fill in the balance of the design. Yellow comma strokes complete the flange detail. PRIVATE COLLECTION

Measuring 9 x 6 inches, this red half-sheet waiter has a narrow semitransparent white band around the floor, which has a crystallized center. The ends of the border design are three large light-medium blue leaves, and the sides are light-medium blue comma-stroke leaves, with red berries all around the design. There is blue striping around the inside of the border, with arched striping on the four corners. A simple yellow stripe is around the middle of the flange. This tray was not painted on the back.

PRIVATE COLLECTION

This unusual half-sheet waiter measuring 9 x 6 inches is completely crystallized on both the floor and flange, with a very transparent copper or asphaltum border around the floor edge and flange. The tray has two thin stripes and a broad yellow one on the floor and one broad yellow stripe around the top edge of the flange. PRIVATE COLLECTION

Opposite: Measuring 12 1/4 x 8 3/4 inches, this one-sheet waiter has an asphaltum background. The semitransparent white border is 2 1/2 inches wide, and the tray floor has a beautiful crystallized center. The design consists of four large yellow flowers, four yellow ochre and moss green leaves with red berries and black linework details, and four moss green and medium blue leaves with red berries and black linework details. Dots and beautifully executed squiggles complement this design. A fine yellow stripe edges the inside white band, and comma strokes enhance the flange. On the back of this tray, many names were scratched into the asphaltum. On the upper flange is the name Paul Root with the date 1925. PRIVATE COLLECTION

Here is a large cut-corner tray, measuring 12 1/4 x 8 1/2 inches. It has an asphaltum background with beautifully executed folk-art flowers of vermilion with red and white overstrokes. The two upper center flowers have fine yellow cross-hatching. Two large green leaves have fine-line yellow details and darker green veins. Green stroke leaves with yellow comma strokes and yellow stems complete the design. A yellow stripe enhances the tray floor, and a triple comma-stroke border is on the flange. The artist's signature is at the bottom right of the design and on the back view of the piece. LANDIS VALLEY MUSEUM COLLECTION

RAYMOND J. SCHNADER
ROHRERSTOWN, PENNA.

Raymond J. Schnader also decorated this black background tray, which measures 12 3/8 x 9 inches and has a double border on the floor. The outer border is white and has vermilion folk-art flowers with yellow overstrokes and black details, green leaves with yellow details for veins, and green berries with yellow details and stems. Black squiggles add to the design. The thin inner band is yellow with fine black strokes and dots. Triple vermilion comma strokes add to the details of the floor. A single row of yellow comma strokes is on the flange.

LANDIS VALLEY MUSEUM COLLECTION

This large black background tray measuring 17 1/4 x 12 1/8 inches has a large central strokework flower with a red base and overstrokes of alizarin crimson and white. Two large green leaves with yellow detail enhance the bottom of the flower, and elongated comma strokes with yellow details form leaves at the top of the flower. A series of red comma strokes with alizarin crimson and white details complements the top of the flower along with a cluster of yellow comma strokes at top center. Notice the yellow cross-hatching and dot flowers. Double fine-line stripes edge the floor of the tray, and the flange has a single row of comma strokes. LANDIS VALLEY MUSEUM COLLECTION

This oblong bread tray has an ashpaltum background with semitransparent white bands on the ends. Four groups of three red cherries with green stroke details for leaves and yellow stroke work design complete the end details. The sides have large S strokes, and there is a fine yellow stripe though the center. The crystallized floor has no strokework or details. PRIVATE COLLECTION

Here is another asphaltum bread tray with a crystallized floor and a white band on each end. The end details are four vermilion ball flowers, each with transparent alizarin crimson overstrokes on the top half and fine black details to denote the flower center. Strokework green leaves and red berries complete the details on the white bands. The ends each have a series of yellow strokes and the sides have alternating vermilion and yellow comma strokes. The floor has a $1/2$-inch yellow stripe around the outside edge, with a fine black wavy line detail.

PRIVATE COLLECTION

This red oblong bread tray measures $12\,3/4$ x $8\,7/8$ inches. The sides each have a cluster of three teardrop strokes, with two dots along the top edge and two comma strokes along the bottom edge. The floor has a white band, with green stylized leaves, red berries, and black linework details. A broad yellow stripe, an inner fine yellow stripe, and comma strokes finish the design.

LANDIS VALLEY MUSEUM COLLECTION

Here is an oval bun dish with an asphaltum background and crystallized floor. The sides have a white band with a variety of vermilion flowers with yellow centers, alizarin crimson overstrokes, and fine black details, along with green leaves with black details. The ends have yellow comma strokes around the top edge of the handholds and yellow with black fine-line details around the lower edge. A $1/2$-inch yellow stripe or band is around the outer edge of the floor, with fine black comma-stroke details. PRIVATE COLLECTION

Measuring 4 1/2 inches tall x 3 inches in diameter, this asphaltum base-coated round spice canister has a variety of vermilion ball flowers, with alizarin crimson and semitransparent white overstrokes. Yellow and green comma strokes form the leaves. A series of three comma strokes forms the border design around the top, and vermilion comma strokes highlight the edge of the cap. PRIVATE COLLECTION

This small oval spice canister measures 4 inches high. It is asphaltum with a beautiful white ball-flower design that includes yellow and vermilion overstrokes with fine black details, along with four white petals with vermilion over strokes. Yellow and green stroke leaves with black veins and three vermilion berries complete the design. Yellow comma strokes are around the top of the canister and lid.

PRIVATE COLLECTION

A border of teardrops and double dots encircles the top of this asphaltum hinged-lid canister. Yellow comma strokes are on the bottom edge. It measures 6 3/4 x 5 1/2 inches. Repeated around the canister are yellow flowers with vermilion finger-painted centers and yellow leaves.

PRIVATE COLLECTION

The focal point of the design on this red oval hinged-lid box is the yellow bird with green wings, reminiscent of the style of bird found on some coffeepots. The box has a dome lid, wire ring handle, and clasp, and it measures 7 inches high, 6 inches deep, and 9 inches long. There are several alizarin crimson flowers with semitransparent white overstrokes and green trim, with yellow dots at the base of each flower. Stylized green leaves with yellow veins and green and yellow comma strokes complete the details. Groupings of comma strokes encircle the sides of the lid, and the dome top has comma strokes around the edge. PRIVATE COLLECTION

This black 4 3/4-inch-high flat-top round canister with hinged lid, ring handle, and clasp has vermilion stroke flowers with green and yellow stroke leaves on the front half only. The yellow S strokes form the edge of the lid's design. The flat top of the lid has a fine yellow stripe around the edge and yellow strokework detail around the ring handle. PRIVATE COLLECTION

This black round tea canister measures 6 1/2 inches tall and 4 1/4 inches wide. It has three ball flowers with alizarin crimson and white overstrokes, along with yellow and green comma strokes for leaves. A yellow stripe encircles both the bottom and top of the canister. The lid has two yellow and green comma strokes, and the rim of the lid has a broad red stripe. This design is the basis for that on the oblong tray in the project section.

RAY AND PAT OXENFORD COLLECTION

Opposite: This round hinged-lid canister has a white band in the center of the front half only. The two views will help you get a better feel for the design. There are large green leaves with black details at both sides, along with three vermilion flowers. The center tuliplike flower has yellow comma strokes with black details, the flower on the left has a yellow overstroke and black details, and the ball flower on the right side has just the black details. Black squiggles and small strokes complete the design. Fine yellow stripes are about an inch above and below the white band, only as long as the band. Comma strokes encircle the bottom edge of the canister, the top flange, and the side drop of the lid. PRIVATE COLLECTION

Featuring a large red ball flower on either side, this red-orange dome-lid sugar bowl has alizarin crimson and semitransparent white overstroke details. Yellow and green comma-stroke leaves complete the design. Yellow comma strokes surround the bottom flange, and the dome lid has four small white ball flowers with red overstroke detail and three yellow comma strokes between each flower. PRIVATE COLLECTION

Here's another red dome-lid sugar bowl. Take note of the different shades of red in these sugar bowls. This one has a dark gray ball flower on both front and back, with yellow and black comma-stroke details. Yellow and green comma strokes form the leaves. The bottom flange has an elongated S stroke for the border, and the dome top has four smaller dark gray ball flowers with yellow and black comma-stroke details. Elongated yellow comma strokes border the edge of the lid. PRIVATE COLLECTION

This asphaltum background sugar bowl has a bronze tint. Note that its lid is slightly different in style, being flat in the center with a large tin ring for the handle. The bottom flange is curved as well. There is a $^3/_4$-inch white band around the top edge of the sides and a $^1/_2$-inch white band around the edge of the lid. Both bands have red berries and green stroke leaves, with fine black lines for details. Three yellow ochre stripes are around the bottom, and the lid and handle have a yellow stripe. RAY AND PAT OXENFORD COLLECTION

Syrup cups are similar in style to creamers, but they have a hinged lid that also covers the pouring spout. This 4 1/2-inch-tall syrup cup has a black background with a semitransparent white shield on each side. A vermilion scalloped-edge flower with yellow center and black details, green leaves, and a yellow comma-stroke border complete the design on each side. A yellow comma stroke is on each side of the spout, and comma-stroke details enhance the lid. PRIVATE COLLECTION

Note the similarity of this black syrup cup to the previous one. It measures 4 1/2 inches high and has a white shield design with a beautiful red folk-art flower with yellow center and black details. Green comma strokes represent the leaves. The shield is enhanced with fine-line details, as well as a fine yellow stripe along the bottom edge. The lid designs are almost identical, with clusters of graduated yellow comma strokes. LANDIS VALLEY MUSEUM COLLECTION

This syrup cup is a little larger than the others are, at 5 inches tall. It has an asphaltum background, and the entire design is yellow comma strokes to form the flowers, leaves, and all details. Notice the fine cross-hatching in the centers of the flowers. Both broad and fine yellow stripes are around the bottom, and a fine yellow stripe is around the top. The lid is enhanced with yellow comma strokes. PRIVATE COLLECTION

Cups and mugs were made in a variety of sizes. This tapered mug has a black background with two vermilion ball flowers and three vermilion berries on each side, along with green and yellow comma-stroke leaves. In the front view, you can faintly see the alizarin crimson stroke detail on the large ball flowers. PRIVATE COLLECTION

Below is an asphaltum mug that is $5^3/_4$ inches high. It has a white band around the top enhanced by strokework folk-art flowers with yellow overstrokes, black details, and green stroke leaves. A fine yellow stripe along with four comma strokes encircle the mug. LANDIS VALLEY MUSEUM COLLECTION

At left, this black background mug is 6 inches tall and 4 inches in diameter and has a semitransparent white band around the top edge. Three scalloped-edge flowers that have yellow centers with black details encircle the top edge of the cup, along with stylized green stroke leaves enhanced by black details. A fine yellow stripe surrounds the bottom edge of the white border, along with yellow comma strokes. PRIVATE COLLECTION

Consisting entirely of yellow comma strokes and a large green rickrack stroke around the top, this red background cup is unusual in its lack of floral designs. Around the top third of the cup are two fine yellow stripes bordering fine green stripes; this same detail appears around the very top edge of the cup. Double comma strokes complement the stripes, and elongated teardrop strokes are around the bottom. PRIVATE COLLECTION

This tin mug has a flange on the bottom and handle. It possibly could have been a personalized shaving mug—note the initials E. J. B. on the center front of the flange. It has a gold scrollwork design with black details or shadow. Several broad and thin gold stripes complete the design. LANDIS VALLEY MUSEUM COLLECTION

The detail on this small vermilion tin tumbler is simply a yellow and green strokework border along the top edge.

PRIVATE COLLECTION

Believed to be from the early 1900s, this large red cup with a white band measures 8 inches in diameter and 4 inches high. Notice the rivets to secure the handle. The white band is overpainted with yellow tuliplike flowers, vermilion flowers and buds, and green and red leaves with black details. The bottom portion has strokework flowers and leaves in yellow.

PRIVATE COLLECTION

Tin miniatures were quite popular and often used for children's toys. This small oblong bread tray measures only 3 1/2 inches long and 1 1/2 inches wide. It has a yellow background with simple dot flowers in white, vermilion, green, and blue for its design on the floor. PRIVATE COLLECTION

Here's another miniature oblong bread tray with a slightly different curve to the sides. This one has a vermilion background with yellow stroke flowers and green strokework leaves. A black stripe outlines the floor.
PRIVATE COLLECTION

This child's coffeepot is 2 3/4 inches tall. It sports a vermilion background with a white flower complemented by overstrokes of transparent alizarin crimson and green stroke leaves on both sides. PRIVATE COLLECTION

Measuring 4 9/16 x 3 inches, this miniature child's tray has a vermilion background, with peachlike design and finger-painted overtones and black details. Green comma strokes for leaves and black fine-line details and strokes complete the floor design. A thin black stripe surrounds the flange.

LANDIS VALLEY MUSEUM COLLECTION

Here are three pieces of children's tinware. The coffeepot is $2^3/8$ inches high, with a vermilion background. Simple white comma strokes with yellow center form the flower, and the leaves are green comma strokes. The bucket measures $4^1/4$ inches high, including the handle, and has a similar design of a white comma-stroke flower with yellow center and green comma-stroke leaves, also on a vermilion background. The tin cup measures $1^7/8$ inches high and has a red background with simple graduated yellow and green comma strokes for the decorative details.

LANDIS VALLEY MUSEUM COLLECTION

This miniature book box with yellow background has two strokework red flowers with green leaves, and a red stripe around the edge. Note the ring handle along the side to open the book. PRIVATE COLLECTION

Document boxes or trunks came in many sizes, from miniature to very large, and a variety of styles, including dome-top, flat-top, and platform-top boxes. Miniature flat-tops were often referred to as shoe-blackening trunks. They could have either wire-ring or brass handles.

This miniature dome-top box measures 3 inches long, 2 inches wide, and 1 3/4 inches tall, with a wire ring for the handle. The base coat is asphaltum with a white band on the front only, along with simple strokes in red and green. The lower yellow stripe goes completely around the box, but the upper yellow stripe is only on the two sides and back. A few yellow strokes complete the lid design around the handle. PRIVATE COLLECTION

This dome-top document box measuring 6 1/4 inches long, 2 3/4 inches wide, and 3 1/2 inches high has an asphaltum base coat with a white band on the front only, with two red-ball and stroke flowers with yellow details, along with yellow and red strokes for leaves. The bottom half of the front is personalized with an initial and last name with decorative striping around the name. The sides and back have a simple yellow stripe. The lid has yellow stroke detail as well. PRIVATE COLLECTION

This dome-top document box with asphaltum base coat measures 9 inches long, $4\frac{1}{2}$ inches wide, and 6 inches high. It has decoration only on the dome top and front—no decorations or striping are on the sides, back, or dome-top sides. The front details are vermilion stroke flowers with alizarin crimson and white overstroke details, along with green strokework leaves with yellow details. A yellow stripe surrounds the front panel, and a double yellow stripe surrounds the dome-top edge. Only a few yellow comma strokes surround the wire-ring handle on the dome top. PRIVATE COLLECTION

The red dome-top document box here measures 9 inches long, $4\frac{1}{2}$ inches wide, and $5\frac{1}{2}$ inches tall. The design is two large and two small red ball flowers, with alizarin crimson and white overstroke details. The large flowers also have yellow cross-hatching and short yellow strokes along the top edges, and the smaller flowers have dots. Large green strokes with smaller yellow strokes form the leaves. The dome top has a black stripe around the edge, with a white rickrack stroke inner border. Each of the four corners of the lid has a cluster of three comma strokes. Comma-stroke detail also appears around the wire-ring handle. The top edges, sides, and back have no details or striping. PRIVATE COLLECTION

Opposite: Here's an exquisite example of a double border on this black-background document box that measures $6\frac{3}{4}$ inches long, 3 inches wide, and $3\frac{1}{2}$ inches high. The front has both opaque white and scalloped red borders. The white border has two red cherries with a black dot and green stroke leaves with black details. Groupings of yellow comma strokes and dots complement the red scallops. The dome top has yellow and red comma strokes on each end and yellow comma strokes along the front and back, as well as a yellow stripe on the inside edge of the design. Comma-stroke details in yellow also surround the ring handle. The front edge of the dome top has five yellow teardrop strokes and double dots, and both ends have clusters of yellow comma strokes. The back has no detail. PRIVATE COLLECTION

Here's another beautifully decorated dome-top document box with ashpaltum base coat. Measuring 10 inches long, 6 1/4 inches wide, and 8 inches high, this box also has a white band along the top edge of the front only. The band has four vermilion stroke flowers with alizarin crimson overstroke details and two large green leaves with black details. A few fine black strokes fill in the empty spaces. Below the white band is a shallow vermilion scallop with comma overstrokes in alizarin crimson and white. The bottom two-thirds of the front has vermilion flowers and berries with alizarin crimson and white details, along with large green leaves and yellow comma-stroke filler leaves. A fine yellow stripe goes around the side and bottom edges of the front. The dome top has a fine double yellow stripe all around, with yellow and vermilion strokes on both ends, and the front and back edges each have four comma strokes. Comma-stroke detail is around the wire-ring handle. Note that the clasp closure is missing on the front of the lid. The close-up of the sides shows the fine double-line stripe on the top and bottom with elongated S strokes with fine-line details. The lid side edges each have a yellow double-line stripe and three comma strokes. There are no details nor striping on the back.

PRIVATE COLLECTION

This large dome-top document box measuring 9 1/2 inches long, 6 1/2 inches wide, and 8 inches high also has an asphaltum background and a white band on the front only. The white border has two comma-stroke flowers with alizarin crimson overstrokes, elegant green stroke leaves, vermilion berries, and graceful flowing black squiggles and details. A fine-line red stripe edges the bottom of the white band. The bottom front design is two ball flowers with alizarin crimson and white overstrokes, plus two vermilion stroke flowers with alizarin crimson and white overstrokes and fine-line yellow cross-hatching in the center. Vermilion berries, green leaves and strokes, with yellow strokes and graceful fine lines complete the details. Along the front sides

beneath the white band and across the bottom is a fine yellow stripe, with a cluster of strokes in each corner of the front. The center front edge of the dome top has a cluster stroke design in yellow, and there are complementary designs on each side. The large center cluster design is repeated on both ends of the document box, along with a double stripe. The bottom edges of the sides also have a double stripe and yellow comma strokes. The dome top has a double fine-line stripe all around, with a cluster of yellow strokes in each corner to complement those on the front. There are elongated fine-line comma strokes around the front, back, and sides. Yellow comma strokes surround the wire-ring handle. PRIVATE COLLECTION

Coffeepots were made in a variety of styles and shapes, including straight spout, straight side spout, and crook or gooseneck. Note the triangular inset pieces or gores beneath the handles, some larger than others. This was necessary to complete the vessel portion of the coffeepot, as the early sheets of tin were not large enough to form the vessel. Some coffeepots had a beading design in the tin, which could be single, double, or triple bead.

The black background straight-spout coffeepot shown here measures 8 1/2 inches tall and 6 inches in diameter. It has a lovely design of two vermilion stroke flowers with alizarin crimson and white overstrokes and a smaller yellow flower with black details. There are two large green leaves with yellow details, along with yellow stroke leaves. A fine yellow stripe encircles the bottom. Around the top edge of the vessel are clusters of three comma strokes. PRIVATE COLLECTION

Here's another straight-spout coffeepot measuring 8 1/2 inches tall and 6 inches in diameter. This pot has an asphaltum base coat with semitransparent white bands on both top and bottom edges of the vessel. Above the bottom white band are flowers and leaves completed in yellow. The details on both white bands are semitransparent; more varnish was added to the pigments for this effect. The fruit and flower details are done in vermilion, light orange, green, and medium blue. Black details complete the design. In the other view, note the usual type of lid handle found on most coffeepots, as well as the beautiful strokework details in yellow. It also allows you to see the opposite side of the coffeepot. PRIVATE COLLECTION

A side-spout coffeepot makes it so easy to pour. This fine example has a black base coat, with the design on the front two-thirds of the vessel. The one small and two large vermilion ball flowers have alizarin crimson and white stroke detail, white cross-hatching, and yellow strokes around the upper edges of the flowers. There are two vermilion berries with alizarin crimson details and yellow dots, as well as green and yellow stroke leaves. You can see in the other view that the back third has only a few yellow comma strokes beneath the spout, while the lid has both yellow strokework and cross-hatching. There is no striping on this coffeepot. Also note the extremely small gore inserted at the bottom edge beneath the handle. PRIVATE COLLECTION

This is another great example of an early side-spout coffeepot with an asphaltum background. The pot measures 8 inches high and 5 inches in diameter. Here again the design is only on two-thirds of the vessel. The design consists of two large ball flowers and four buds in vermilion, with alizarin crimson overstroke details and yellow dots for the flower centers. Elongated yellow and green comma strokes form the delicate leaf composition, and yellow cross-hatching is between the two center flowers. A yellow stripe encircles the bottom, and elongated teardrop strokes form the top border. In the other view, notice the intricate yellow strokework details both beneath and on the underside of the side spout. The lid has complex yellow strokework details, along with two vermilion strokes. PRIVATE COLLECTION

This gooseneck coffeepot sports an asphaltum base coat. The design is painted on a white semitransparent circle. There are two vermilion and yellow flowers with black trim and a third flower of vermilion, yellow, and light blue with black details. Yellow comma strokes encircle the white circle. The upper yellow border is $^3/_4$ inch wide, with fine black comma strokes and red dots. Yellow rickrack strokes are on the bottom flange, and a fine yellow stripe is just above the flange. The lid has a single row of yellow comma strokes on the edge and several yellow comma strokes flowing out from the brass knob. PRIVATE COLLECTION

Compared to the previous gooseneck coffeepots, this red-background gooseneck coffeepot has a spout that is slightly flared out. Also note the small circles of tin to form the knob on the lid of this coffeepot. The handle does not include the extra piece usually used to help strengthen it. The design includes two large red ball flowers with alizarin crimson and white overstrokes, plus yellow dots for the details, and both yellow and green comma strokes to represent the leaves. The bottom flange has red rickrack strokes with yellow dots on the flange and a double row of yellow strokes around the top edge. The other view shows the details of the strokework on the lid.

PRIVATE COLLECTION

The background color on this very unusual gooseneck coffeepot is a blue-black, and the intricate flower designs are different on each side. Note the high dome lid and its large knob. The curve to the handle is slightly different, and there is a triple beading design in the vessel near the top. On this side, the red petals come to the center to form the flower, which is outlined in yellow. Stylized green leaves and graceful yellow curved lines complete the details. Note the double row of red strokes down the front of the spout. The other view shows a red flower formed by an oval with smaller petals of varying sizes around the outside edge and a double bud in red. Both the flower and buds have fine yellow details. Similar stylized green leaves and graceful yellow curved lines complete the details. A simple fine yellow stripe goes around the center of the bottom flange. A double row of red strokes encircles the top of the vessel, and red strokes radiate out from the large knob on the lid. PRIVATE COLLECTION

This red gooseneck coffeepot measures $10\,^3/_4$ inches tall. Most of the original design is gone, but you can tell that the central folk-art flower was made from multiple comma strokes. There are three small ball flower buds above the flower and comma-stroke leaves. A ball flower bud and comma strokes are on each side of the main flower, and two stylized leaves composed of multiple comma strokes enhance the bottom of the flower. You can still see the yellow comma stroke details and some of the white over-strokes on the central flower. Double comma strokes encircle the bottom flange, top edge of the vessel, and rim of the lid. Four comma strokes complete the design on the inner portion of the lid.

LANDIS VALLEY MUSEUM COLLECTION

This large red basin with sloped sides measures 12 inches in diameter and 5 inches high. On the inside of the upper edge, it has a $2^3/8$-inch semitransparent white band with yellow peaches that have finger-painting shading details, deep red leaves with black details, and blue berries. Around the circular base are yellow comma-stroke clusters, and yellow comma-stroke details surround the upper edge of the outside of this basin. PRIVATE COLLECTION

Match safes were very popular items. This style was most commonly made, although there were slight variations. This open wall match safe measures $7^1/2$ inches high x 4 inches wide, with an asphaltum base coat. Simple comma strokes in yellow and red with green overstrokes complete the design. On the V-shaped bottom are S strokes in red and green, along with striping in yellow and red. Yellow comma strokes are on both sides of the bottom. PRIVATE COLLECTION

This large oval black tub measuring 19 inches long, 14 inches wide, and $8^1/2$ inches deep has rope handles on each side. It has a large central vermilian flower with yellow center and details, along with smaller pale yellow flowers with yellow centers, four large vermilion buds, and several smaller vermilion berries, green leaves, and yellow comma-stroke details. The tub in made in four sections, and a fine red stripe outlines each of these sections. PRIVATE COLLECTION

This black-background oil filler pot that measures 8 1/4 inches high and 6 1/4 inches wide at the base has a large red flower with comma-stroke petals with yellow overstrokes and dots. On both sides are green and yellow comma strokes representing the leaves, along with yellow dots. The top edge has six elongated red comma strokes with clusters of three yellow comma strokes. The top edge of the raised opening and the end of the thin spout are encircled in red. The handle also has red teardrop strokes with yellow dots. There are clusters of yellow comma strokes under the spout and toward the back of the handle at the bottom edge. A variation of this design was often painted on gooseneck coffeepots as well. RAY AND PAT OXENFORD COLLECTION

This ornate tin cradle has a red-orange background with a large yellow daisy-like flower on the side that is shown, along with a green leafy vine. The flower on the opposite side is different, but it also has a green leafy vine. The inside head end of the cradle appears to have had two stripes, although all traces of the paint are missing. The painted details are no longer on the foot end either, but the outline remaining gives the indication that a bird of some sort with a plume tail may have been painted there. There is also green to represent grass.

PRIVATE COLLECTION

This unusual black-background apple dish has a semi-transparent yellow background on each of the four sides that does not entirely cover them but comes to within 1/4 inch of each edge. Four identical all-over designs consist of three vermilion flowers with a single alizarin crimson stroke on each, three clusters of four yellow berries with black details, and green leaves with black details. Short black strokes and dots fill in the empty spaces. A thin yellow strip surrounds each of the four sections. The square base has fine yellow stroke and dot details. RAY AND PAT OXENFORD COLLECTION

From the 1920s through mid 1950s, several companies produced tinware serving trays in various sizes and styles that were reproductions of the eighteenth- and nineteenth-century English and French trays.

This green tray measures 17 1/4 inches long x 14 3/16 inches wide. It has violets and leaves, with a gold band around the outside edge.

RANDY AND FAITH WESTLEY COLLECTION

This black-background tray measures 17 1/4 inches long x 14 3/16 inches wide. It has a folk-art rose, daisy, smaller flowers, and leaves. Gold strokework and stripe around the edge complete the design. Notice the signature of the artist in the lower right corner; this was a feature of Nashco Products of New York. The company's label can be seen in the second view showing the back of the tray.

RANDY AND FAITH WESTLEY COLLECTION

This green tray measures 13 inches wide x 19 3/4 inches long, including the handles. It also has feet on the back. Here again, stylized folk-art flowers and leaves are the theme of the design. A gold elongated S stroke forms the border. Note the label on the reverse side indicating that the tray was hand-painted in Philadelphia. My mother received this tray as a Christmas gift from my father in the early 1950s, and it was used only on special occasions.

RAY AND PAT OXENFORD COLLECTION

SUPPLIES AND RESOURCES

Ace Hardware Corporation
866-920-5334
www.acehardware.com

A. C. Moore
www.acmoore.com
Paints, brushes, art supplies

Artist's Club
800-845-6507
www.ArtistsClub.com
Paints, brushes, miscellaneous supplies, books,
pattern packets

Chroma Inc. USA
205 Bucky Dr.
Lititz, PA 17543
717-626-8866
www.chromaonline.com
Manufacturer of the JoSonja's
paints and mediums

Dick Blick Art Materials
P.O. Box 1267
Galesburg, IL 61402-1267
800-447-8192
www.dickblick.com

The Home Depot
800-553-3199
www.homedepot.com

JoSonja's
2136 Third St.
Eureka, CA 95501
888-567-6652
www.josonja.com
Books, pattern packets, brushes, seminars

Lowe's Home Improvement
800-445-6937
www.lowes.com

Michael's
www.michaels.com
Paints, brushes, art supplies

Museum Books, Inc.
Larry Ward, President
P.O. Box 5977
Wyomissing, PA 19610
610-372-0642
museumbooks@1usa.com
out-of-print books

Ray Oxenford
805 Hill Dr.
Douglassville, PA 19518
(610) 385-3431
paoxenford@dejazzd.com
Tinsmith: traditional reproduction tinware, repairs

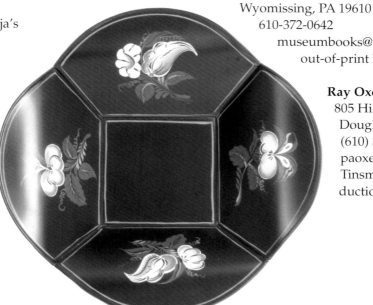

The pattern for this apple dish was designed by Pat Oxenford from a small picture. The flowers are white with semitransparent details in vermilion, light blue, and black. Green leaves have yellow and black details, and there is a yellow stripe around all sections of the dish sides and floor.

This black warmer measures 10 inches high and 4 inches in diameter. The simple decoration consists of a pale blue stroke flower with yellow center and a vermilion stroke flower with yellow center. Green leaves with yellow detail complete the design. PRIVATE COLLECTION

Parker Paints, Inc.
610-396-9763
www.shadesof76.com
Shades of '76 oil and latex paints

Scharff Brushes, Inc.
P.O. Box 746
Fayetteville, GA 30214
888-SCHARFF, 770-461-2200
SCHARFF@ARTBRUSH.com
www.ARTBRUSH.com
Brushes and quills

Steph's Folk Art Studio
Monica Renninger, Owner
Spruce Lane Cottages
2439 Old Philadelphia Pike
P.O. Box 99
Smoketown, PA 17576
800-510-3193, 717-299-4973
Paints, brushes, painting supplies, pattern packets, books, classes, tin

Utrecht Art Supplies
6 Corporate Dr.
Cranbury, NJ 08512
www.utrecht.com
All types of painting and art supplies

ORGANIZATIONS

Historical Society of Early American Decoration
HSEAD, Inc., at the Farmers' Museum
P.O. Box 30
Cooperstown, NY 13326
866-304-7323
www.HSEAD.org

Society of Decorative Painters
393 N. McLean Blvd.
Wichita, KS 67203-5968
316-269-9300

This 5¹/₂-inch-tall red spice canister sports four vermilion ball flowers with alizarin crimson and white comma overstrokes. The top and bottom ball flowers are decorated the same, and the right and left ball flowers are decorated the same. Yellow and green comma strokes complete the details, and the top of the canister has yellow comma-stroke details. LANDIS VALLEY MUSEUM COLLECTION

MUSEUMS, HISTORIC SITES, AND FESTIVALS

Many museums and historic sites in southeastern Pennsylvania and surrounding areas have specialized collections of Pennsylvania Dutch folk art, including painted tinware. Many have specific hours of operation, so it's best to call ahead to make an appointment or find out what hours they are open to the public.

Abby Aldrich Rockefeller Folk Art Museum
325 W. Francis St.
Williamsburg, VA 23185

American Folk Art Museum
45 W. 53rd St.
New York, NY 10019
212-265-1040
www.folkartmuseum.org

Historical Society of Berks County
940 Center Ave.
Reading, PA 19601
610-375-4375
www.berkshistory.org

Kutztown Folk Festival
Kutztown Fairgrounds
Kutztown, PA
888-674-6136
www.kutztownfestival.com
One of America's oldest and most popular folklife festivals, held during the first week of July each year. Many skilled artisans, including tole painters, offer Pennsylvania Dutch crafts for sale and demonstrate how they are made, following the traditional methods used by their forefathers.

Landis Valley Museum
2451 Kissel Hill Rd.
Lancaster, PA 17601
717-569-0401
www.landisvalleymuseum.org
Many well-preserved buildings in a village setting and a very large collection of artifacts. Hosts several special events throughout the year on Pennsylvania Dutch customs and sponsors summer and winter institutes on traditional crafts.

Mennonite Heritage Center
565 Yoder Rd.
Harleysville, PA 19438-1020
215-256-3020
www.mhep.org

Pennsylvania German Cultural Heritage Center at Kutztown University
22 Luckenbill Rd.
Kutztown, PA 19530
610-683-1589
www.kutztown.edu/community/pgchc

Reading Public Museum
500 Museum Rd.
West Reading, PA 19611
610-371-5850
www.readingpublicmuseum.org

Schwenkfelder Library and Heritage Center
105 Seminary St.
Pennsburg, PA 18073-1898
215-679-3103
www.schwenkfelder.com

Winterthur Museum
Route 52
Winterthur, DE 19735
800-448-3883
www.winterthur.org

BIBLIOGRAPHY

BOOKS

Brazer, Esther Stevens. *Early American Decoration*. Springfield, MA: Pond-Ekberg, 1940. Reprint, 1961.

Coffin, Margaret. *The History and Folklore of American Country Tinware, 1700–1900*. New York: Galahad Books, 1968.

Cramer, Edith. *Handbook of Early American Decoration*. Boston: Charles T. Branford, 1951. Reprint, 1968.

De Francesco, Italo L. *Design Motif: The (Art of the) Pennsylvania Germans*. Sandusky, OH: Prang, 1947.

Hutchings, Dorothy Dean. *A Quarter Century of Decorating and Teaching Country Painting*. Tucson, AZ: Shandling Lithographing, 1975.

Jansen, Jo Sonja. *Jo Sonja's Guide to Decorative Painting: Traditional Inspirations—Contemporary Expressions*. New York: Watson-Guptill Publications, 1999.

Kauffman, Henry J. *Pennsylvania Dutch American Folk Art*. Rev. ed. Elverson, PA: Self-published, 1993.

Lichten, Frances. *Folk Art of Rural Pennsylvania*. New York: Bonanza Books, n.d.

Martin, Gina, and Lois Tucker. *American Painted Tinware: A Guide to Its Identification*. 4 vols. New York: Historical Society of Early American Decoration, 1997–2007.

Richardson, Nancy. *How to Stencil and Decorate Furniture and Tinware*. New York: Ronald Press, 1956.

Slayton, Mariette Paine. *Early American Decorating Techniques*. New York: Macmillan, 1972, 1979.

Stacks, Clyde P. *Pennsylvania Dutch Folk Art: Designs for Decorating*. Palmyra, PA: Self-published, n.d.

Zook, Jacob and Jane. *How to Paint and Decorate Furniture and Tinware*. Paradise, PA: Self-published, 1960.

VIDEOS

Expression of Common Hands: Folk Art of the Pennsylvania Dutch. Washington, DC: New River Media, 1998.

HSEAD Masters Series: Traditional Country Painting. With Lois Tucker. Cooperstown, NY: Historical Society of Early American Decoration, 2003